· SERMONS ON ·
# THE SECOND COMING OF CHRIST

· SERMONS ON ·
# THE SECOND COMING OF CHRIST

![Hendrickson Publishers]

**Sermons on the Second Coming of Christ**

© 2016 Hendrickson Publishers Marketing, LLC
P. O. Box 3473
Peabody, Massachusetts 01961-3473

ISBN 978-1-61970-755-9

All rights reserved. No part of this book may be reproduced or transmitted in any form or by any means, electronic or mechanical, including photocopying, recording, or by any information storage and retrieval system, without permission in writing from the publisher.

Originally published by Hendrickon Publishers in *Sermons on The Last Days*.

*Printed in the United States of America*

Cover photo of Charles Haddon (C. H.) Spurgeon by Herbert Rose Barraud is used by permission of the University of Minnesota Libraries, Special Collections and Rare Books.

# Contents

| | |
|---|---|
| Preface | vii |
| An Awful Premonition | 1 |
| The Reward of the Righteous | 15 |
| The Great White Throne | 29 |
| The Great Assize | 43 |
| Jesus Admired in Them That Believe | 55 |
| The Ascension and the Advent Practically Considered | 70 |
| Coming Judgment of the Secrets of Men | 84 |
| The Two Appearings and the Discipline of Grace | 98 |
| The Watchword for Today: "Stand Fast" | 112 |
| "He Cometh with Clouds" | 126 |
| Preparation for the Coming of the Lord | 140 |
| Watching for Christ's Coming | 154 |
| Index to Key Scriptures | 164 |

*In memory of Patricia Klein (1949–2014), our colleague and friend, who spent her life caring for words and who edited this series. She is truly missed.*

# Preface

## Charles Haddon Spurgeon
## 1834–1892

Ask most people today who Charles Haddon Spurgeon was, and you might be surprised at the answers. Most know he was a preacher, others remember that he was Baptist, and others go so far as to remember that he lived in England during the nineteenth century. All of this is true, yet Charles Haddon Spurgeon was so much more.

Born into a family of Congregationalists in 1834, Spurgeon's father and grandfather were both Independent preachers. These designations seem benign today, but in the mid-nineteenth century, they describe a family committed to a Nonconformist path—meaning they did not conform to the established Church of England. Spurgeon grew up in a rural village, a village virtually cut off from the Industrial Revolution rolling over most of England.

Spurgeon became a Christian at a Primitive Methodist meeting in 1850 at age sixteen. He soon became a Baptist (to the sorrow of his mother) and almost immediately began to preach. Considered a preaching prodigy—"a boy wonder of the fens"—Spurgeon attracted huge audiences and garnered a reputation that reached throughout the countryside and into London. As a result of his great success, Spurgeon was invited to preach at the New Park Street Chapel in London in 1854, when he was just nineteen. When he first preached at the church, they were unable to fill even two hundred seats. Within the year, Spurgeon filled the twelve-hundred-seat church to overflowing. He soon began preaching in larger and larger venues, outgrowing each, until finally in 1861 the Metropolitan Tabernacle was completed, which seated six thousand persons. This would be Spurgeon's home base for the rest of his career, until his death in 1892 at age fifty-seven.

Spurgeon married Susannah Thompson in 1856 and soon they had twin sons, Charles and Thomas, who would later follow him in his work. Spurgeon opened Pastors' College, a training school for preachers, which trained over nine hundred preachers during his lifetime. He also opened orphanages for underprivileged boys and girls, providing education to each of the orphans. And with Susannah, he developed a program to publish and distribute Christian literature. He is said to have preached to over ten million people in his forty years of ministry. His sermons sold over twenty-five thousand copies each week and were translated into twenty languages. He was utterly committed to spreading the gospel through preaching and through the written word.

During Spurgeon's lifetime, the Industrial Revolution transformed England from a rural, agricultural society to an urban, industrial society, with all the attendant difficulties and horrors of a society in major transition. The people displaced by these sweeping changes—factory workers and shopkeepers—became Spurgeon's congregation. From a small village himself and transplanted to a large and inhospitable city, he was a common man and understood innately the spiritual needs of the common people. He was a communicator who made the gospel so relevant, who spoke so brilliantly to people's deepest needs, that listeners welcomed his message.

Keep in mind that Spurgeon preached in the days before microphones or speakers; in other words, he preached without benefit of amplifier systems. Once he preached to a crowd of over twenty-three thousand people without mechanical amplification of any sort. He himself was the electrifying presence on the platform: he did not stand and simply read a stilted sermon. Spurgeon used an outline, developing his themes extemporaneously, and speaking "in common language to common people." His sermons were filled with stories and poetry, drama and emotion. He was larger than life, always in motion, striding back and forth across the stage. He gestured broadly, acted out stories, used humor, and painted word pictures. For Spurgeon, preaching was about communicating the truth of God, and he would use any gift at his disposal to accomplish this.

Spurgeon's preaching was anchored in his spiritual life, a life rich in prayer and the study of Scripture. He was not tempted by fashion, be it theological, social, or political. Scripture was the cornerstone of Spurgeon's life and his preaching. He was an expositional preacher mostly, exploring a passage of Scripture for its meaning both within the text as well as in the lives of each member of his congregation. To Spurgeon, Scripture was alive and specifically relevant to people's lives, whatever their social status, economic situation, or time in which they lived.

One has a sense that Spurgeon embraced God's revelation completely: God's revelation through Jesus Christ, through Scripture, and through his own prayer and study. For him, revelation was not a finished act: God still reveals himself, if one made oneself available. Some recognize Spurgeon for the mystic he was, one who was willing and eager to explore the mysteries of God, able to live with those bits of truth that do not conform to a particular system of theology, perfectly comfortable with saying, "This I know, and this I don't know—yet will I trust."

Each of the sermons in this collection was preached at a different time in Spurgeon's career and each has distinct characteristics. These sermons are not a series, as they were not created or intended to be sequential, nor have they been homogenized or edited to sound as though they are all of a kind. Instead, they reflect the preacher himself, allowing the voice of this remarkable man to ring clearly as he guides the reader into a particular account, a particular event—to experience, with Spurgeon, God's particular revelation.

As you read, *listen*. These words were meant to be heard, not merely read. Listen carefully and you will hear the cadences of this remarkable preaching, the echoes of God's timeless truth traveling across the years. And above all, enjoy Spurgeon's enthusiasm, his fire, his devotion, his zeal to recognize and respond to God's timeless invitation to engage the Creator himself.

# An Awful Premonition

~~~

Delivered at the Metropolitan Tabernacle, Newington. No. 594.

*Verily I say unto you, There be some standing here, which shall not taste of death, till they see the Son of man coming in his kingdom.*
—MATTHEW 16:28

I must confess that I have frequently read this verse with but a vague sense of its profound impressiveness, and I have passed it over rapidly because I did not understand it clearly. Though well acquainted with the usual interpretations, none of them had ever satisfied my mind. It seemed to me as if the text had awakened surprise without suggesting a simple obvious meaning, and therefore the good commentators had invented explanations and offered suggestions, widely different one from another, but all equally obscure and improbable. Lately, however, in reading a volume of sermons by Bishop Horsley, I have met with altogether a new view of the passage, which I firmly believe to be the correct one. Though I do not suppose I shall carry the judgment of all of you with me, yet I shall do my best to bring out of it that terrible denunciation which I believe the Savior has here left on record. With his own cross and passion in view, he was admonishing his disciples to steadfastness, appealing to them at any sacrifice to take up their cross and follow him; then portraying the inestimable value of the soul and reflecting on the horror of the soul being lost—a doom, the full force of which, it would be impossible to comprehend until he should come in the glory of his Father, with all his holy angels—he stopped short, looked upon some of the company, and said in words like these, "There are certain persons standing here who shall never taste of death, till they see the Son of man coming in his kingdom."

Now what did he mean by this? Obviously it is either a marvelous promise to some who were his disciples indeed, or else it is a portent of woe to others who should die in their sins. How do the popular interpretations of our learned expositors look at it?

Some say it refers to the transfiguration, and it certainly is remarkable that the account of the transfiguration immediately follows this verse, both in Mark and in Luke, as well as in this record of Matthew. But can you for a moment bring your minds to believe that Christ was describing his transfiguration when he spoke of "the Son of man coming in his kingdom," and whether you can see any connection between the transfiguration and the preceding verse, which says, "For the Son of man shall come in the glory of his Father with his angels; and then he shall reward every man according to his works"? We grant you that Christ was in his glory upon Mount Tabor, but he did not there "reward every man according to his works," nor is it fair to call that a "coming" of the Son of man at all. He did not "come" on Mount Tabor, for he was on the earth already; and it is a misuse of language to construe that into an advent. Besides, where would be the occasion for such a solemn prefix, "Verily I say unto you"? Does it not raise expectation merely to cause disappointment, if he intended no more than this, "There be some standing here who shall see me transfigured"? That scene took place six days afterward. The next verse tells you so, "And after six days Jesus takes Peter, James, and John his brother, and brings them up into a high mountain apart." Why, the majesty of the prediction which carries our thoughts forward to "the last things" in the world's history makes us shrink from accepting an immediate fulfillment of it all. I cannot imagine, therefore, that the transfiguration is in the slightest degree referred to here; and I do not think that anyone would have thought of such a thing unless he had been perplexed and utterly nonplussed for an explanation.

And again—though it seems almost incredible—Dr. Gill endorses this view, and moreover says, that it also refers to the descent of the Holy Ghost. At this I am staggered. How any man can find an analogy with Pentecost in the connection here I cannot think. Pentecost took place six months after this event, and why Jesus Christ should say, "Verily I say unto you, there be some standing here who will live six months," I really cannot comprehend. It seems to me that my Master did not waste people's time by talking such platitudes. Who that reads this passage can think it has any reference to the descent of the Holy Ghost, "For the Son of man shall come in the glory of his Father with his angels; and then shall he reward every man according to his works"? Did Christ come at Pentecost in the glory of his Father? Was there then any company of angels? Did he then reward every man according to his works? Scarcely can the descent of the Holy Spirit, or the appearance of cloven tongues, like as of fire, be called the "coming of the Son of man in the glory of his Father with his angels, to give every man according to his works," without a gross misuse of our mother tongue, or a strange violation of symbolic imagery.

Both these constructions, however, which I now mention, have now been given up as unsatisfactory by those modern students who have thought most carefully upon the subject. The third still holds its ground and is currently received, though I believe it to be quite as far from the truth as the others. Will you carefully read the chapter through at your leisure, and see if you can find anything about the siege of Jerusalem in it? Yet this is the interpretation that finds favor at the present time. Some persons were standing there who would be alive when Jerusalem should be destroyed by the Romans! Nothing surely could be more foreign to the entire scope of our Lord's discourse, or the narrative of the evangelists. There is not the slightest shadow of a reference to the siege of Jerusalem. It is the coming of the Son of man which is here spoken of, "in the glory of his Father with his angels, to reward men according to their works." Whenever Jesus spoke of the siege of Jerusalem and of its coming, he was inclined to say, "Verily I say unto you, this generation shall not pass till all these things be fulfilled"; but he never singled out some few persons and said to them, "Verily I say unto you, there be some standing here, which shall not taste of death, till the city of Jerusalem is besieged and destroyed."

If a child were to read this passage, I know what he would think it meant: he would suppose Jesus Christ was to come, and there were some standing there who should not taste of death until really and literally he did come. This, I believe, is the plain meaning.

"Well," says one, "I am surprised; do you think, then, that this refers to the apostle John?" No; by no means. The fable passed current, you know, that John was to live till Christ came again. But John himself repudiated it. For at the end of his gospel, he says, "Then went this saying abroad among the brethren, that that disciple should not die: yet Jesus said not unto him, 'He shall not die'; but, 'If I will that he tarry till I come, what is that to thee?'" This, you see, was putting a suppositious case, and in no sense the language of prediction.

Now, dear brethren, if you are so far convinced of the unreasonableness of each of these efforts to solve the difficulty by feigning a sense, I shall hope to have your minds in readiness for that explanation which appears to me to harmonize with every requirement. I believe the "coming" here spoken of is the coming of the Son of God to judgment at the last great and terrible assize, when he shall judge the righteous and separate the wicked from among them.

The next question is, "Of whom were the words spoken?" Are we warranted in supposing that our Lord intended this sentence as a gracious promise, or a kindly expectation that he would kindle in the breast of his disciples? I think not. To me it appears to have no reference whatever to any man who ever had grace in his soul: such language is far more applicable to the ungodly than the wicked. It may well have been aimed directly at those followers who should apostatize from the faith, grasp at the world, shrink at the cross, endeavor to save their lives, but really lose them, and barter their souls. At the glorious appearing of Christ there are some who will taste death, but will they be the righteous? Surely, my dear friends, when Christ comes, the righteous will not die; they will be caught up with the Lord in the air. His coming will be the signal for the resurrection of all his saints. But mark you, at the time of his coming, the men who have been without God, and without Christ, will begin for the first time to "taste of death." They passed the first stage of dissolution when the soul quit the body, but they have never known the "taste of death." Till then, they will not have known its tremendous bitterness and its awful horror. They will never drink of the wormwood and the gall, so as really to "taste of death," till the Lord shall come. This tasting of death here may be explained, and I believe it is to be explained, by a reference to the second death, which men will not taste of till the Lord comes. And what a dreadful sentence that was, when the Savior said—perhaps singling out Judas as he spoke, "Verily I say unto you, there be some standing here, who shall never know what that dreadful word 'death' means, till the Lord shall come. You think that if you save your lives, you escape from death. Ah! you do not know what death means. The demise of the body is but a prelude to the perdition of the soul. The grave is but the porch of death; you will never understand the meaning of that terrible word till the Lord comes." This can have no reference to the saints, because in the eighth chapter of John, and the fifty-first verse, you find this passage, "Verily, verily, I say unto you, 'If a man keep my saying, he shall never see death.' Then said the Jews unto him, 'Now we know that thou hast a devil. Abraham is dead, and the prophets; and thou sayest, "If a man keep my saying, he shall never taste of death."'" No righteous man, therefore, can ever "taste of death." He will fall into that deep oblivious sleep in which the body sees corruption; but that is another and a very different thing from the bitter cup referred to as tasting of death. When the Holy Ghost wanted an expression to set forth that which was the equivalent for the divine wrath, what expression was used? "Christ, by the grace of God, tasted death for every man." The expression "to taste of death" means the reception of that true and essential death, which kills both the body and the soul in hell forever. The Savior said then, as he might say, I fear, if he stood in this pulpit tonight, "Verily I say unto you, There be some standing here, which shall not taste of death, till they see the Son of man coming in his kingdom."

If this be the meaning, and I hold that it is in keeping with the context, it explains the verse, sets forth the reason why Christ bespoke breathless attention with the word "verily," answers both the grammar and the rhetoric, and is not by any argument that I have ever heard of to be moved—if this be so, what thrilling denunciations are contained in my text. Oh, may the Holy Spirit deeply affect our hearts and cause our souls to thrill with its solemnity!

What thoughts it stirs up! Compared with the doom which will be inflicted upon the ungodly at the coming of Christ, the death of nature is nothing. We go farther: compared with the doom of the wicked at the coming of Christ, even the torments of souls in a separate state are scarcely anything. The startling question then comes up. Are there any sitting or standing here who will have to taste of death when the Lord comes?

## 1. The sinner's death is but a faint presage of the sinner's doom at the coming of the Son of man in his glory.

Let me endeavor to show the contrast. We can make but little comparison between the two *in point of time*. Many men meet with their death so suddenly that it can scarcely involve any pain to them. They are crushed, perhaps, by machinery; a shot sends them to find a grave upon the battlefield; or they may be speedily poisoned. If they be for hours, or days, or weeks, or months, upon the bed of sickness, yet the real work of dying is but short. It is rather a weary sort of living than an actual sense of dying while hope lingers though even in fitful dreams. Dying is but the work of a moment: if it shall be said to last for hours, yet the hours are brief. Misery may count them long, but oh! with what swift wings do they fly! To die, to fall asleep, to suffer, it may be but a pin's prick, and then to have passed away from the land of the living to the realm of shades! But oh! the doom which is to be brought upon the wicked when Christ comes! This is a death which never dies. Here is a heart palpitating with eternal misery. Here is an eye never filmed by the kind finger of generous forgetfulness. Here will be a body never to be stiffened in apathy; never to be laid quietly in the grave, rid of keen pangs, wearing disease, and lingering wretchedness. To die, you say, is nature's kind release: it brings ease. It comes to a man, for this world at least, a farewell to his woes and griefs; but there shall be no ease, no rest, no pause in the destination of impenitent souls. "Depart, ye cursed," shall ever ring along the endless aisles of eternity. The thunderbolt of that tremendous word shall follow the sinner in his perpetual flight from the presence of God; from its baleful influence he shall never be able to escape; no, never. A million years shall make not so much difference to the duration of his agony as a cup of water taken from the sea would to the volume of the ocean. No, when millions of years told a million times shall have rolled their fiery orbits over his poor tormented head, he shall be no nearer to the end than he was at first. Talk of *death*! I might even paint him as an angel when once I think of the terrors of the wrath to come. Soon come, soon gone is death. That sharp scythe gives but one cut, and down falls the flower and withers in the heat of the sun; but eternity, eternity, eternity, who shall measure its wounds, who shall fathom the depths of the gashes? When eternity wields the whip, how dreadfully will it fall! When eternity grasps the sword, how deep shall be the woundings, how terrible its killing!

> *To linger in eternal pain,*
> *Yet death forever fly.*

You are afraid of death, sinner; you are afraid of death; but were you wise, you would be ten thousand times ten thousand times more afraid of the coming and the judgment of the Son of man.

In point of loss there is no comparison. When the sinner dies it is not tasting of death in its true sense, for what does he lose? He loses wife, and children, and friends; he loses all his dainty bits and his sweet drafts. Where now his viol and his lute? Where now the merry dance and the joyful company? For him no more the pleasant landscape nor the gliding stream. For him no more the light of the sun by day, nor the light of moon and stars by night. He has lost at one stroke every comfort and every hope. But then the loss, as far as death is concerned, is but a loss of earthly things, the loss of temporal and temporary comforts, and he might put up with that. It is wretched enough to lose these, but let your imagination follow me, faint as is my power to describe the everlasting and infinite loss of the man who is found impenitent at the last great judgment day. What loses he then? The harps of heaven and the songs thereof; the joys of God's presence and the light thereof; the jasper sea and the gates of pearl. He has lost peace and immortality and the crown of life; no, he has lost all hope, and when a man has lost that, what remains to him? His spirit sinks with a terrible depression, more frightful than maniac ever knew in his wildest moods of grief. His soul sinks never to recover itself into the depths of dark despair, where not a ray of hope can ever reach him. Lost to God; lost to heaven; lost to time; lost to the preaching of the gospel; lost to the invitation of mercy; lost to the prayers of the gracious; lost to the mercy seat; lost to the blood of sprinkling; lost to all hope of every sort; lost, lost, forever! Compared with this loss, the losses of death are nothing, and well might the Savior say, that lost spirits shall not even "taste of death" until he shall come, and they shall receive their sentence.

Neither does death bear any comparison with the last judgment *in point of terror*. I do not like to paint the terrors of the deathbed of unawakened men. Some, you know, glide gently into their graves. It is, in fact, the mark of the wicked that they have no bands in their death: but their strength is firm; they are not troubled like other men are. Like the sheep they are laid in the grave. A peaceful death is no sign of grace. Some of the worst of men have died with a smile upon their countenance to have it changed for one eternal weeping. But there are more men of other exquisite sensibility, instructed men, who cannot die like brutes, and they have alarms and fears and terrors when they are on their deathbeds. Many an atheist has cried to God under dying pangs, and many an infidel who heretofore could brag and speak high things against God has found his cheek turn pale and his throat grow hoarse when he has come there. Like the mariner, the boldest man in that great storm reels to and fro and staggers like a drunken man and is at his wits' ends; for he finds that it is no child's play to die. I try sometimes to picture that hour, when we shall perhaps be propped up in the bed or lying down with pillows round about us, be diligently watched; and as they hush their footfalls and gaze anxiously on, there is a whisper that the solemn time has come, and then there is a grappling of the strong man with the stronger than he. Oh! what must it be to die without a Savior, to die in the dark without a light except the lurid glare of the wrath to come! Horrors there are, indeed, around the deathbed of the wicked, but these are hardly anything compared with the terrors of the day of judgment. When the sinner wakes from his bed of dust, the first object he will see will be the great white throne and the Judge seated upon it: the first sound that will greet his ears will be the trumpet sounding—

*Come to judgment, come to judgment,*
*Come to judgment, sinner, come.*

He will look up, and there will be the Son of man on his judgment throne, the King's officers arranged on either side, the saints on his right hand, and angels round about; then the books will be opened. What creeping horror will come upon the flesh of the wicked man! He knows his turn will arrive in a moment; he stands expecting it; fear takes hold upon him, while the eyes of the Judge look him through and through, and he cries to the rocks to hide him, and the mountains to fall upon him. Happy would he be now to find a friendly shelter in the grave, but the grave has burst its doors, and can never be closed upon him again. He would even be glad to rush back to his former state in hell, but he must not. The judgment has come, the assize is set; again the trumpet rings—

*Come to judgment, come to judgment,*
*Come to judgment, come away.*

And then the book is opened, and the dread sentence is pronounced; and, to use the words of Scripture, "Death and hell are cast into the lake of fire. This is the second death. And whosoever was not found written in the book of life was cast into the lake of fire." The man never knew what death was before. The first death was but a flea bite; this is death indeed. The first death he might have looked back upon as a dream, compared with this tasting of death now that the Lord has come.

From what we can glean darkly from hints of Scripture, *the pains of death* are not at all comparable to the pains of the judgment at the second advent. Who will speak in a depreciating manner of the pains of death? If we should attempt to do so, we know that our hearts would contradict us. In the shades of night, when deep sleep falls upon men, you sometimes suddenly awake. You are alarmed. The terror by night has come upon you. You expect—you hardly know what it is, but you are half afraid that you are about to die. You know how the cold sweat comes upon the brow. You may have a good hope through grace, but the very thought of death brings a peculiar pang. Or when death has really come in view, some of us have marked with terrible grief the sufferings of our dearest friends. We have heard the eye-strings break; we have seen the face all pallid, and the cheek all hollow and sunken. We have sometimes seen how every nerve has become a road for the hot feet of pain to travel on, and how every vein has been a canal of grief. We have marked the pains and moans and groans and dying strife that fright the soul away. These, however, are common to man. Not so the pangs which are to be inflicted both on body and on soul at the coming of the Son of God; they are such that I cast a veil over them, fearful of the very thought. Let the Master's words suffice, "Fear him who is able to cast both body and soul into hell; yea, I say unto you, fear him." Then the body in all the parts shall suffer; the members which were once instruments of unrighteousness shall now be instruments of suffering. And the mind, the major sinner, shall be also the greater sufferer. The memory, the judgment, the understanding, the will, the imagination, and every power and passion of the soul become a deep lake of anguish. But I spare you these things; oh! spare yourselves! God alone knows with what pain I discourse upon these horrors. Were it not that they must be spoken of, or else I must give my account at the day of judgment as a faithless servant; were it not that I speak of them in mercy to your souls, poor sinners, I would fain forget them altogether, seeing that my own soul has a hope in him who saves from the wrath to come. But as long as you will not have mercy upon yourselves, we must lay this ax at your root; so long as you will make a mock of sin and set at naught the terrors of the world to come, we must warn you of hell. If it be hard to *talk* of these things, what must it be to *endure* them? If a dream makes you quiver from head to foot, what must it be to endure really, and in person, the wrath to come? O souls, were I to speak as I ought, my knees would knock together with trembling now; were you to feel as you should, there would not be an unconverted man among you who would not cry, "Sirs, what must I do to be saved?" I do conjure you to remember that death, with all its pangs, is but a drop of a bucket compared with the deep, mysterious, fathomless, shoreless sea of grief you must endure forever at the coming of the Lord Jesus except you repent.

Death makes great discoveries. The man thought himself wise, but death draws the curtain, and he sees written up in large letters, "Thou fool!" He said he was prudent, for he hoarded up his gold and silver and kept the wages of the laborer; but now he finds that he has made a bad bargain, while the question is propounded to him, "What doth it profit thee, to have gained the world, and to have lost thy soul?" Death is a great revealer of secrets. Many men are not believers at all until they die; but death comes, and makes short work with their skepticism. It gives but one blow upon the head of doubt, and all is done; the man believes then, only he believes too late. Death gives to the sinner the discovery that there is a God, an angry God, and punishment is wrapped up in the wrath to come. But how much greater the discoveries that await the day of judgment! What will the sinner see then? He will see the man who was crucified sitting upon the throne. He will hear how Satan has been defeated in all his craftiest undertakings. Read from those mysterious books, the secrets of all hearts shall then be revealed. Then men shall understand how the Lord reigned supremely even when Satan roared most loudly; how the mischief and the folly of man did but after all bring forth the great purposes of God. All this shall be in the books, and the sinner shall stand there defeated, terribly defeated, worsted at every point, baffled, foiled, stultified in every act and every purpose by which he thought to do well for himself; yes, and utterly confounded in all the hostility and all the negligence of his heart toward the living and true God who would and who did rule over him. Too late, he will discover the preciousness of the blood he despised, the value of the Savior he rejected, the glory of the heaven which he lost, the terror of the hell to which he is sentenced. How wise, how dreadfully wise will he be when fully aware of his terrible and eternal destruction! Thus sinners shall not taste of death in the real meaning of the term, until the Lord shall come.

**2. Still further**—*in the state of separate spirits they have not fully tasted of death, nor will they do so until Christ comes.*

The moment that a man dies, his spirit goes before God. If without Christ, that spirit then begins to feel the anger and the wrath of God. It is as when a man is taken before a magistrate. He is known to be guilty, and therefore he is remanded and put in prison till his trial shall come. Such is the state of souls apart from the body: they are spirits in prison, waiting for the time of their trial. There is not, in the sense in which the Romanist teaches it, any purgatory; yet there is a place of waiting for lost spirits which is in Scripture called "hell," because it is one room in that awful prison house in which must dwell forever spirits that die finally impenitent and without faith in Christ. But those of our departed countrymen and fellow citizens of earth who die without Christ have not yet fully tasted of death, nor can they until the advent of the Lord.

Just consider why not. *Their bodies do not suffer.* The bodies of the wicked are still the prey of the worm; still the atoms are the sport of the winds and are traversing their boundless cycles, and must do so until they are gathered up into the body again, at the trump of the archangel—at the voice of God.

The ungodly know that their present state is to have an end at the judgment, but after the judgment their state will have no end; it is then to go on, and on, and on, forever and forever, unchanged and unchangeable. Now there may be half a hope, an anticipation of some change, for change brings some relief; but to the finally damned, upon whom the sentence has been pronounced, there is no hope even of a change. Forever and forever shall there be the same ceaseless wheel of misery.

The ungodly, too, in their present state, have not as yet been put to the shame of a public sentence. They have, as it were, merely been cast into prison, the facts being too clear to admit of any doubt as to the sentence, and they are their own tormentors, vexing and paining themselves with the fear of what is yet to come. They have never yet heard that dreadful sentence, " Depart, ye cursed, into everlasting fire, prepared for the devil and his angels."

I was struck while studying this subject, to find how little is said about the pains of the lost while they are merely souls, and how much is said concerning this when the Lord comes. You have that one parable of the rich man and Lazarus, and there it speaks of the soul being already tormented in the flame; but if you turn to the thirteenth chapter of Matthew, and read the parable of the tares, you will find it is at the end of the world that the tares are to be cast into the fire. Then comes the parable of the dragnet. It is when the dispensation comes to an end that the net is to be dragged to shore, and then the good are to be put in vessels, and the bad cast away; and then the Lord says, "The Son of man shall send forth his angels, and they shall gather out of his kingdom all things that offend, and them which do iniquity; and shall cast them into a furnace of fire: there shall be wailing and gnashing of teeth." That memorable description in Matthew of those of whom he said, "I was an hungered, and ye gave me no meat; I was thirsty, and ye gave me no drink," is described as happening when the "Son of man shall come in his glory, and all his holy angels with him." The apostle Paul, too, tells us plainly in the Epistle to the Thessalonians, that the wicked are to be destroyed at his coming by the brightness of his power. The recompense of the ungodly, like the reward of the righteous, is anticipated now: but the full reward of the righteous is to be at his coming; they are to reign with Christ; their fullness of bliss is to be given them when the King himself in his glory shall sit upon his throne. So, too, the wicked have the beginning of their heritage at death, but the dread fullness of it is to be hereafter.

At the present moment, death and hell are not yet cast into the lake of fire. Death is still abroad in the world slaying men; hell is yet loose; the devil is not yet chained, but still does he go about the "dry places, seeking rest, and finding none." At the last day, at the coming of Christ, "death and hell shall be cast into the lake of fire." We do not understand the symbol; but if it means anything, one would think it must mean this, that at that day the scattered powers of evil, which are to be the tormentors of the wicked, but which have thus far been wandering up and down throughout the world, shall all be collected together, and then, indeed, shall it be that the wicked shall begin to "taste of death" as they have never tasted of it before!

My soul is bowed down with terror while I speak these words to you. I scarcely know how to find suitable words to express the weight of thought which is upon me. My dear hearers, instead of speculating upon these matters, let us try to shun the wrath to come; and what can help us to do that better than to weigh the warning words of a dear and loving Savior, when he tells us that at his coming such a doom shall pass upon impenitent souls, that compared with it, even death itself shall be as nothing? Christians, by the faith of their risen Lord, swallow death in victory; but if you die impenitent, you swallow death in ignorance. You do not feel its bitterness now. But oh! that bitter pill has yet to work its way, and that fierce draft has yet to be drained even to the dregs, unless you repent.

And now, does not the meditation of these terrors prompt *a question?* Jesus said, "Verily I say unto you, there be some standing here, which shall not taste of death, till they see the Son of man coming in his kingdom." *Are there any standing or sitting here who shall not taste of death till then?*

In that little group addressed by the Savior stood Judas. He had been trusted by his Master, and he was an apostle, but after all he was a thief and a hypocrite. He, the son of perdition, would not taste of death till Christ should come in his kingdom. Is there a Judas here? I look into your faces, and many of you are members of this church, and others of you I doubt not are members of other Christian churches, but are you sure that you have made sound work of it? Is your religion genuine? Do you wear a mask, or are you an honest man? O sirs, try your own hearts, and since you may fail in the trial, ask the Lord to search you; for as the Lord my God lives, unless you thus search yourselves and find that you are in the right, you may come presumptuously to sit at the Lord's table. Though with a name to live, you may be among his people here, you will have to taste of death when the Lord comes. You may deceive *us*, but you cannot deceive *him*. The preacher reflects that he himself may be mistaken, that he himself may be self-deceived. If it be so, may the Lord open his eyes to know the worst of his own state. Will you put up this prayer for yourselves, professors? Do not be too bold, you who say you are Christ's; never be satisfied till you are quite sure of it; and the best way to be sure is to go again just as you went at first, and lay hold on eternal life through the power of the blessed Spirit, and not by any strength of your own.

No doubt, however, there stood in that little throng around the Savior some who were careless sinners. He knew that they had been so during the whole of his teaching, and that they would be so still, and therefore they would taste of death at his coming. Are there not some careless persons come in here tonight? I mean you who never think about religion, who generally look upon the Sunday as a day of pleasure, or who loll about in your shirt-sleeves nearly all the day; you who look upon the very name of religion as a bugbear to frighten children with; who mock at God's servants, and contemn the very thought of earnestly seeking after the most High. Oh! will you, will you be among the number of those who taste of death when the Son of man shall come in his kingdom? Oh! must I ring your death knell tonight? Must my warning voice be lost upon you? I beseech you to recollect that you must either *turn* or *burn*. I beseech you to remember this, "Let the wicked forsake his way and the unrighteous man his thoughts; and let him turn unto the Lord, and he will have mercy upon him; and to our God, for he will abundantly pardon." By the wounds of Jesus, sinner, stop and think. If God's dear Son was slain for human sin, how terrible must that sin be! And if Jesus died, how base are you if you are disobedient to the doctrine of faith! I pray you if you think of your body, give some thought to your soul. "Wherefore do ye spend money for that which is not bread? and your labor for that which satisfieth not?" Hearken diligently unto Jehovah's Word, and eat of that which is good, real, and substantial food. Come to Jesus, and your soul shall live.

And there are some here of another class, Bethsaida sinners, Capernaum sinners. I mean some of you who constantly occupy these pews and stand in yonder area and sit in yonder gallery Sunday after Sunday. The same eyes look down on me week after week; the same faces salute me often with a smile when the Sabbath comes, and I pass you journeying to this the tabernacle of your worship, and yet how many of you are still without God and without Christ! Have I been unfaithful to you? If I have, forgive me, and pray to God both for me and for yourselves that we may mend our ways. But if I have warned you of the wrath to come, why will you choose to walk in the path which leads to it? If I have preached to you Christ Jesus, how is it that his charms move you not, and that the story of his great love does not bring you to repentance? Oh, that the Spirit of God would come and deal with you, for I cannot. My hammer breaks not your flinty hearts, but God's arm can do it, and oh, may he turn you yet. Of all sinners over whom a minister ought to weep, you are the worst; for while the careless perish, you perish doubly. You know your Master's will, and yet you do it not. You see heaven's gate set open, and yet you will not enter. Your vicious free will ruins you; your base and wicked love of self and sin destroys you. "Ye will not come unto me that ye might have life," said Christ. You are so vile that you will not turn even though Jesus should woo you. I do pray you let the menace of judgment to come contained in my text, stir you now if you have never been stirred before. May God have pity on you even if you will have no pity upon yourselves.

Peradventure among that company there were some who held the truth, but who held it in licentiousness—and there may be such here present. You believe in the doctrine of election, so do I; but then you make it a cloak for your sin. You hold the doctrine of the perseverance of the saints, but you still persevere in your iniquity. Oh! there is no way of perishing that I know of worse than perishing by making the doctrines of grace an excuse for one's sins. The apostle has well said of such that their damnation is just: it is just to any man, but to a sevenfold degree is it just to such as you are. I would not have you forget the doctrine, nor neglect it, nor despise it, but I do beseech you do not prostitute it, do not turn it to the vile purposes of making it pander to your own carnal ease. Remember, you have no evidence of election except you are holy, and that you have no right to expect you will be saved at the last unless you are saved now. A present faith in a present Savior is the test.

Oh, that my Master would bring some of you to trust him tonight. The plan of salvation is simple. Trust Christ, and you are saved; rely upon him, and you shall live. This faith is the *gift of God,* but remember that though God gives it, he works in you to will and to do of his own good pleasure. God does not believe for you; the Holy Spirit does not believe for you; you must believe, or else you will be lost: and it is quite consistent with the fact that it is the gift of God, to say that it is also the act of man. You must, poor soul, be led to trust the Savior, or into heaven you can never enter. Is there one here who says, "I would find the Savior tonight"? Go not to your bed until you have sought him, and seek you him with sighs and with tears.

I think this is a night of grace. I have preached the law and the terrors of the Lord to you, but it will be a night of grace to the souls of some of you. My Master does but kill you that he may make you alive; he does but wound you that he may make you whole. I feel a sort of inward whisper in my heart that there are some of you who even now have begun your flight from the wrath to come. Whither do you flee? Fly to Jesus. Haste, sinner, haste. I trust you will find him before you retire to your beds, or if you lie tossing there in doubt and fear, then may he manifest himself unto you before the morning light. I think I would freely give my eyes if you might but see Christ, and that I would willingly give my hands if you might but lay hold on him. Do, I conjure you, put not from you this warning, but let it have its proper work upon you and lead you to repentance. May God save you, and may the prayer we have already offered this evening be answered, that the company of you may be found among his elect at his right hand. To that end, let us pray.

Our Father, save us with your great salvation. We will say unto God, do not condemn us; deliver us from going down to the pit, for you have found the ransom; may we not be among the company that shall taste of death when the Son of man shall come. Hear us, Jesus, through your blood. God be merciful to us sinners. Amen.

# The Reward of the Righteous

~⊙~

Delivered on Sunday morning, January 21, 1866, at the Metropolitan Tabernacle, Newington. No. 671.

*When the Son of man shall come in his glory, and all the holy angels with him, then shall he sit upon the throne of his glory: and before him shall be gathered all nations: and he shall separate them one from another, as a shepherd divideth his sheep from the goats: and he shall set the sheep on his right hand, but the goats on the left. Then shall the King say unto them on his right hand, "Come, ye blessed of my Father, inherit the kingdom prepared for you from the foundation of the world: for I was an hungered, and ye gave me meat: I was thirsty, and ye gave me drink: I was a stranger, and ye took me in: naked, and ye clothed me: I was sick, and ye visited me: I was in prison, and ye came unto me." —*MATTHEW 25:31–36

It is exceedingly beneficial to our souls to mount above this present evil world to something nobler and better. The cares of this world and the deceitfulness of riches are apt to choke everything good within us, and we grow fretful, desponding, perhaps proud, carnal. It is well for us to cut down these thorns and briars, for heavenly seed sown among them is not likely to yield a harvest, and I do not know a better sickle with which to cut them down than thoughts of the kingdom to come. In the valleys in Switzerland, many of the inhabitants are deformed and dwarfish, and the whole of them wear a sickly appearance, for the atmosphere is charged with miasma, and is close and stagnant; you traverse them as rapidly as you can, and are glad to escape from them. Up yonder on the mountain, you will find a hardy race, who breathe the clear fresh air as it blows from the virgin snows of the Alpine summits. It would be well for their frames if the dwellers in the valley could frequently leave their abodes among the marshes and the fever mists and get themselves up into the clear atmosphere above. It is to such an exploit of climbing that I invite you this morning. May the Spirit of God bear us as upon eagles' wings, that we may leave the mists of fear and the fevers of anxiety, and all the ills which gather in this valley of earth, and get ourselves up to the mountains of future joy and blessedness where it is to be our delight to dwell world without end! Oh, may God disentangle us now for a little while, cut the cords that keep us here below, and permit us to mount! We sit, some of us, like chained eagles fastened to the rock, only that, unlike the eagle, we begin to love our chain and would, perhaps, if it came really to the test, be loath to have it snapped. May God now grant us grace if we cannot at once escape from the chain of mortal life as to our bodies, yet to do so as to our spirits; and leaving the body like a servant at the foot of the hill, may our soul, like Abraham, go to the top of the mountain, and there may we have communion with the most High.

While expounding my text, I shall ask your attention this morning, first, *to the circumstances which surround the rewarding of the righteous;* second, *to their portion;* and third, *to the persons themselves.*

## 1. There is *much of teaching in the surrounding circumstances.*

We read, "When the King shall come in his glory." It appears, then, that we must not expect to receive our reward till by and by. Like the hireling we must fulfill our day, and then at evening we shall have our penny. Too many Christians look for a present reward for their labors, and if they meet with success, they begin doting upon it as though they had received their recompense. Like the disciples who returned saying, "Lord, even the devils are subject unto us," they rejoice too exclusively in present prosperity; whereas the Master bade them not to look upon miraculous success as being their reward, since that might not always be the case. "Nevertheless," said he, "rejoice not in this, but rather rejoice because your names are written in heaven." Success in the ministry is not the Christian minister's true reward: it is an earnest, but the wages still wait. The approbation of your fellowmen you must not look upon as being the reward of excellence, for often you will meet with the reverse; you will find your best actions misconstrued, and your motives ill interpreted. If you are looking for your reward *here,* I may warn you of the apostle's words, "If in this life only we have hope, we are of all men most miserable," because other men get their reward; even the Pharisee gets his: "Verily, I say unto you, they have their reward"; but we have none here. To be despised and rejected of men is the Christian's lot. Among his fellow Christians he will not always stand in good repute. It is not unmitigated kindness nor unmingled love that we receive even from the saints. I tell you, if you look for your reward to Christ's bride herself, you will miss it; if you expect to receive your crown from the hand even of your brethren in the ministry who know your labors, and who ought to sympathize with your trials, you will be mistaken. "When the King shall come in his glory," then is your time of recompense; but not today nor tomorrow nor at any time in this world. Reckon nothing which you acquire, no honor which you gain, to be the reward of your service to your Master; that is reserved to the time "when the King shall come in his glory."

Observe with delight the august person by whose hand the reward is given. It is written, "When the King shall come." Brethren, we love the King's courtiers; we delight to be numbered with them ourselves. It is no mean thing to do service to him whose head, "Though once 'twas crowned with thorns, is crowned with glory now." But it is a delightful thought that the service of rewarding us will not be left to the courtiers. The angels will be there, and the brethren of the King will be there; but heaven was not prepared by them, nor can it be given by them. Their hands shall not yield us a coronation; we shall join their songs, but their songs would be no reward for us; we shall bow with them and they with us, but it will not be possible for them to give us the recompense of the reward—that starry crown is all too weighty for an angel's hand to bring, and the benediction all too sweet to be pronounced, even by seraphic lips. The King himself must say, "Well done, good and faithful servant." What say you to this, my dear brother? You have felt a temptation to look to God's servants, to the approbation of the minister, to the kindly look of parents, to the word of commendation from your fellow worker; all these you value, and I do not blame you; but these may fail you, and therefore never consider them as being the reward. You must wait till the time when the King comes, and then it will neither be your brethren, your pastors, your parents, nor your helpers, but the King himself who shall say to you, "Come, you blessed." How this sweetens heaven! It will be Christ's own gift. How this makes the benediction doubly blessed! It shall come from his lips, which drop like myrrh and flow with honey. Beloved, it is Christ who became a curse for us, who shall give the blessing to us. Roll you this as a sweet morsel under your tongues.

The character in which our Lord Jesus shall appear is significant. Jesus will then be revealed as truly "the King." "When the King shall come." It was to him as King that the service was rendered, and it is from him as King that the reward must therefore come; and so upon the very threshold a question of self-examination arises: "The King will not reward the servants of another prince—am I therefore his servant? Is it my joy to wait at the threshold of his gates, and sit like Mordecai at the courts of Ahasuerus—at the entrance of his door? Say, soul, do you serve the King?" I mean not the kings and queens of earth; let them have loyal servants for their subjects; but saints are servants of the Lord Jesus Christ, the King of kings—are you so? If you be not so, when the King comes in his glory, there can be no reward for you. I long in my own heart to recognize Christ's kingly office more than ever I have done. It has been my delight to preach to you Christ dying on the cross, and "God forbid that I should glory, save in the cross"; but I want for my own self to realize him on his throne, reigning in my heart, having a right to do as he wills with me, that I may get to the condition of Abraham, who, when God spoke, though it was to tell him to offer up his own Isaac, never asked a question, but simply said, "Here am I." Beloved, seek to know and feel the controlling power of the King, for else when he comes, since you have not known him as King, he cannot know you as servant; and it is only to the servant that the King can give the reward which is spoken of in the text, "When the King shall come."

Now pass on. "When the King shall come in his *glory*." The fullness of that it is impossible to conceive.

*Imagination's utmost stretch,*
*In wonder dies away.*

But this we know—and it is the sweetest thing we can know—that if we have been partakers with Jesus in his shame, we also shall be sharers with him in the luster which shall surround him. Are you, beloved, one with Christ Jesus? Are you of his flesh and of his bones? Does a vital union knit you to him? Then you are today with him in his shame; you have taken up his cross, and gone with him without the camp bearing his reproach; you will doubtless be with him when the cross is exchanged for the crown. But judge yourself this morning; if you are not with him in the regeneration, neither will you be with him when he shall come in his glory. If you start back from the black side of communion, you shall not understand its bright, its happy period, when the King shall come in his glory and all his holy angels with him. What, are angels with him? And yet he took not up angels, he took up the seed of Abraham. Are the holy angels with him? Come, my soul, then you cannot not be far from him. If his friends and his neighbors are called together to see his glory, what do you think if you are married to him? Shall you be distant? Though it be a day of judgment, yet you cannot be far from that heart which having admitted angels into intimacy has admitted you into union. Has he not said to you, O my soul, "I have betrothed thee unto me in faithfulness, and in judgment, and in righteousness"? Have not his own lips said it, "I am married unto thee, and my delight is in thee"? Then if the angels, who are but the friends and the neighbors, shall be with him, it is abundantly certain that his own beloved Hephzibah, in whom is all his delight, shall be near to him and shall be a partaker of his splendor. It is when he comes in his glory, and when his communion with angels shall be distinctly recognized, it is then that his unity with his church shall become apparent. *"Then shall he sit upon the throne of his glory."* Here is a repetition of the same reason why it should be your time and my time to receive the reward from Christ if we be found among his faithful servants. When *he* sits upon his throne it were not fit that his own beloved ones should be in the mire. When he was in the place of shame, they were with him, and now he is on the throne of gold they must be with him too. There were no oneness, union with Christ were a mere matter of talk, if it were not certain that when he is on the throne they shall be upon the throne too.

But I want you to notice one particular circumstance with regard to the time of the reward. It is *when he shall have divided the sheep from the goats.* My reward, if I be a child of God, cannot come to me while I am in union with the wicked. Even on earth you will have the most enjoyment of Christ when you are most separated from this world: rest assured, although the separated path does not seem an easy one, and it will certainly entail upon you persecution and the loss of many friends, yet it is the happiest walking in the world. You conforming Christians, who can enter into the world's mirth to a certain degree, you cannot, you never can know as you now are, the inward joys of those who live in lonely but lovely fellowship with Jesus. The nearer you get to the world, the further you must be from Christ, and I believe the more thoroughly a bill of divorce is given by your spirit to every earthly object upon which your soul can set itself, the more close will be your communion with your Lord. "Forget also thine own country and thy Father's house; so shall the King greatly desire thy beauty, for he is thy Lord, and worship thou him." It is significant that not until the King has separated the sheep from the goats does he say, "Come, ye blessed"; and though the righteous will have enjoyed a felicity as disembodied spirits, yet as risen from the grave in their bodies, their felicity is not fully accomplished till the great Shepherd shall have appeared to separate them once for all, by a great gulf which cannot be passed, from all association with the nations that forget God. Now then, beloved, these circumstances all but together come to this, that the reward of following Christ is not today, is not among the sons of men, is not from men, is not even from the excellent of the earth, is not even bestowed by Jesus while we are here, but the glorious crown of life which the Lord's grace shall give to his people is reserved for the second advent, "when the King shall come in his glory, and all his holy angels with him." Wait with patience, wait with joyful expectation, for he shall come, and blessed be the day of his appearing.

## 2. We have now to turn to the second point—*the portion itself.*

Every word is suggestive. I shall not attempt to exhaust, but merely to glance at all. The reward of the righteous is set forth by the loving benediction pronounced to them by the Master, but *their very position* gives some foreshadowing of it. He put the sheep on his right hand. Heaven is a position of the most elevated dignity authoritatively conferred, and of divine complacency manifestly enjoyed. God's saints are always at his right hand according to the judgment of faith, but hereafter it shall be more clearly manifested. God is pleased to be close to his people, and to place them near to himself in a place of protection. Sometimes it seems as if they were at the left hand; they certainly have, some of them, less comfort than the worldlings. "I have seen the wicked in great power, and spreading himself like a green bay tree; their eyes stand out with fatness, they have more than heart could wish"; whereas his people are often made to drink waters of less than a full cup, and their meat and their drink are bittered with wormwood and gall. The world is upside down now; the gospel has begun to turn it the right way uppermost, but when the day of grace is over, and the day of glory comes, then shall it be righted indeed; then those that wandered about in sheepskins and goatskins shall be clothed in glittering apparel, being transfigured like the Savior upon Tabor; then those of whom the world was not worthy shall come to a world that shall be worthy of them; then those who were hurried to the stake and to the flames shall triumph with chariots of fire and horses of fire, and swell the splendor of the Master's pompous appearing. Yes, beloved, you shall eternally be the object of divine complacency, not in secret and unmanifested communion, but your state and glory shall be revealed before the sons of men. Your persecutors shall gnash their teeth when they see you occupying places of honor at his right hand, and themselves, though greater far than you on earth, condemned to take the lowest room. How shall Dives bite his fire-tormented tongue in vain as he sees Lazarus, the beggar on the dunghill, made to sit at the right hand of the King eternal and immortal! Heaven is a place of dignity. "There we shall be as the angels," says one, but I know that we shall be even superior than they. Is it not written of him who in all things is our representative, "Thou hast put all things under his feet"! Even the very seraphs themselves so richly blessed, what are they but "ministering spirits sent forth to minister to the heirs of salvation"?

But now turning to the welcome uttered by the Judge: the first word is "come." It is the gospel symbol. The law said "go"; the gospel says "come." The Spirit says it in invitation; the bride says it in intercession; "let him that hears" say it by constantly, laboriously endeavoring to spread abroad the good news. Since Jesus says, "Come," we learn that the very essence of heaven is communion. "Come!" You came near enough to say, "Lord, we believe, help thou our unbelief!" On the cross you looked to me and were lightened. You had fellowship with me in bearing my cross. You filled up that which was behind of the sufferings of Christ for his body's sake, which is the church. Still come! Ever, come! Forever, come! Come up from your graves, you risen ones! Come up from among the ungodly, you consecrated ones! Come up from where you cast yourselves down in your humiliation before the great white throne! Come up to wear my crown and sit with me upon my throne! Oh, that word has heaven lurking within it. It shall be to you your joy forever to hear the Savior say to you, "Come." I protest before you my soul has sometimes been so full of joy that I could hold no more when my beloved Lord has said "Come" to my soul; for he has taken me into his banqueting house, and his love-banner has waved over my head, and he has taken me away from the world, and its cares and its fears, and its trials and its joys, up to "the top of Amana, from the top of Shenir and Hermon," where he manifested himself to me. When this "Come" shall come into your ear from the Master's lips, there shall not be the flesh to drag you back, there shall be no sluggishness of spirit, no heaviness of heart; you shall come eternally then; you shall not mount to descend again, but mount on and on in one blessed excelsior forever and forever. The first word indicates that heaven is a state of communion—"come."

Then it is *"Come, ye blessed,"* which is a clear declaration that this is a state of happiness. They cannot be more blessed than they are. They have their hearts' desire, and though their hearts have been enlarged and their desires have been expanded by entering into the Infinite, and getting rid of the cramping influences of corruption and of time, yet even when their desire shall know no bound, they shall have all the happiness that the utmost stretch of their souls can by any possibility conceive. This much, and this is all we know—they are supremely blessed. Their blessedness you perceive does not come from any secondary joy, but from the great primary Source of all good. "Come, ye blessed of my Father." They drink the unadulterated wine at the winepress itself, where it joyously leaps from the bursting clusters; they pluck celestial fruits from the unwithering boughs of the immortal tree; they shall sit at the wellhead and drink the waters as they spring with unrivaled freshness from the depths of the heart of Deity; they shall not be basking in the beams of the sun, but they shall be like Uriel, the angel in the sun; they shall dwell in God, and so their souls shall be satisfied with favor and full and more than full with his presence and benediction.

Notice, once again, that according to the words used it is a state where they shall recognize their right to be there; a state therefore of perfect freedom, and ease and fearlessness. It is *"inherit the kingdom."* A man does not fear to lose that which he wins by descent from his parent. If heaven had been the subject of earning, we might have feared that our merits had not really deserved it, and therefore suspect that one day a writ of error would be issued and that we should be ejected; but we do know whose sons we are; we know whose love it is that makes glad our spirits, and when we "inherit" the kingdom we shall enter it not as strangers or as foreigners, but as sons coming to their birthright. Looking over all its streets of gold and surveying all its walls of pearl we shall feel that we are at home in our own house and have an actual right, not through merit but through grace, to everything that is there. It will be a state of heavenly bliss; the Christian shall feel that law and justice are on his side, and that those stern attributes have brought him there as well as mercy and loving-kindness. But the word "inherit" here imports full possession and enjoyment. They have inherited in a certain sense before, but now as an heir, when he has arrived at full maturity, begins to spend his own money, and to farm his own acres, so do they enter into their heritage. We are not full grown as yet, and therefore are not admitted to full possession. But wait awhile; those gray hairs show, my brethren, that you are getting ripe. These, these, these my still youthful locks show me, alas, that I may have to tarry for a little longer, and yet I know not, the Lord may soon permit me to sleep with my fathers; but later or earlier, be it as he wills, we shall one day come into possession of the good land. Now if it is sweet to be an heir while you are in nonage, what is it to be an heir when arrived at perfect manhood? Was it not delightful to sing that hymn just now, and to behold the land of pure delight, whose everlasting spring and never-withering flowers are just across the narrow stream of death. O you sweet fields! You saints immortal who lie down therein! When shall we be with you and be satisfied? If the mere thinking of heaven ravishes the soul, what must it be to be there, to plunge deep into the stream of blessedness, to dive and find no bottom, to swim and find no shore? To sip of the wine of heaven as we sometimes do makes our hearts so glad that we know not how to express our joy; but what will it be to drink deep and drink again, and sit forever at the table and know that the feast will never be over and the cups will never be empty, and that there will be no worse wine to be brought out at the last, but if possible better still and better still in infinite progression?

The word "kingdom," which stands next, indicates the richness of the heritage of saints. It is no petty estate, no alms rooms, no happy corner in obscurity. I heard a good man say he should be content to win a corner behind the door. I shall not be. The Lord says we shall inherit a *kingdom*. We would not be satisfied to inherit less, because less than that would not suit our character. "He hath made us kings and priests unto God," and we must reign forever and ever, or be as wretched as deposed monarchs. A king without a kingdom were an unhappy man. If I were a poor servant, an alms room would be a boon, for it would consort with my condition and degree; but if I am made by grace a king, I must have a kingdom, or I shall not have attained to a position equal to my nature. He who makes us kings will give us a kingdom to fit the nature which he has bestowed upon us. Beloved, do strive after, more and more, that which the Spirit of God will give you, a kingly heart; do not be among those who are satisfied and contented with the miserable nature of ordinary humanity. A child's glass bead is all the world is to a truly royal spirit; these glittering diadems are only nursery toys to God's kings; the true jewels are up there; the true treasury wealth looks down upon the stars. Do not stint your soul; be not straitened! Get a kingly heart—ask the King of kings to give it to you, and beg of him a royal spirit. Act royally on earth toward your Lord, and for his sake toward all men. Go about the world not as mean men in spirit and act, but as kings and princes of a race superior to the dirt-scrapers who are on their knees, crawling in the mud after yellow earth. Then, when your soul is royal, remember with joy that your future inheritance shall be all that your kingly soul pants after in its most royal moments. It will be a state of unutterable richness and wealth of soul.

According to the word "prepared," we may conceive it to be a condition of surpassing excellence. It is a *kingdom prepared,* and it has been so long a time prepared, and he who prepares it is so wondrously rich in resources, that we cannot possibly conceive how excellent it must be. If I might so speak, God's common gifts, which he throws away as though they were but nothing, are priceless; but what will be these gifts upon which the infinite mind of God has been set for ages of ages in order that they may reach the highest degree of excellence? Long before Christmas chimes were ringing, mother was so glad to think her boy was coming home, after the first quarter he had been out at school, and straightway she began preparing and planning all sorts of joys for him. Well might the holidays be happy when mother had been contriving to make them so. Now in an infinitely nobler manner, the great God has prepared a kingdom for his people; he has thought, "that will please them, and that will bless them, and this other will make them superlatively happy." He prepared the kingdom to perfection; and then, as if that were not enough, the glorious man Christ Jesus went up from earth to heaven; and you know what he said when he departed, "I go to prepare a place for you." We know that the infinite God can prepare a place fitting for a finite creature, but the words smile so sweetly at us as we read that Jesus himself, who is a man, and therefore knows our hearts' desires, has had a finger in it; he has prepared it too. It is a kingdom prepared for *you,* upon which the thoughts of God have been set to make it excellent "from before the foundation of the world."

But we must not pause: it is a "kingdom prepared for *you.*" Mark that! I must confess I do not like certain expressions which I hear sometimes, which imply that heaven is prepared for some who will never reach it; prepared for those who will be driven as accursed ones into the place of torment. I know there is a sacred expression which says, "let no man take thy crown"; but that refers to the crown of ministerial success, rather than of eternal glory. An expression which grated on my ear the other evening, from the lips of a certain good man, ran something in this fashion: "There is a heaven prepared for all of you, but if you are not faithful you will not win it. There is a crown in heaven laid up for you, but if you are not faithful it will be without wearer." I do not believe it, I cannot believe it. That the crown of eternal life, which is laid up for the blessed of the Father, will ever be given to anybody else or left without possessor, I do not believe. I dare not conceive of crowns in heaven and nobody to wear them. Think you that in heaven, when the whole number of saints is complete, you will find a number of unused crowns? "Ah! what are these for? Where are the heads for these?" "They are in hell!" Then, brother, I have no particular desire to be in heaven, for if all the family of Christ are not there, my soul will be wretched and forlorn because of their sad loss, because I am in union with them all. If one soul that believed in Jesus does not get there, I shall lose respect for the promise and respect for the Master too; he must keep his word to every soul that rests on him. If your God has gone the length of actually preparing a place for his people and has made provision for them and been disappointed, he is no God to me, for I could not adore a disappointed God. I do not believe in such a God. Such a being would not be God at all. The notion of disappointment in his eternal preparations is not consistent with Deity. Talk thus of Jupiter and Venus if you please, but the infinite Jehovah is, as far as human speech can dishonor him, dishonored by being mentioned in such a connection. He has prepared a place for you. Here is personal election. He has made a distinct ordinance for every one of his people that where he is there shall they be.

"Prepared from before the foundation of the world." Here is eternal election appearing before men were created, preparing a crown before heads were made to wear it. And so God had before the starry skies began to gleam carried out the decree of election in a measure which when Christ shall come shall be perfected to the praise of the glory of his grace, "who worketh all things after the counsel of his will." Our portion then is one prepared from all eternity for us according to the election of God's grace, one suitable to the loftiest character to which we can ever attain, which will consist in nearness to Christ, communion with God, and standing forever in a place of dignity and happiness.

**3. And now I have very little time to speak, as I hoped to have spoken this morning about** *the persons who shall come there.*

They are recognizable by a secret and by a public character. Their *name* is "blessed of the Father"—the Father chose them, gave his Son for them, justified them through Christ, preserved them in Christ Jesus, adopted them into the family, and now accepted them into his own house. Their nature you have described in the word "inherit." None can inherit but sons; they have been born again, and have received the nature of God; having escaped the corruption which is in the world through lust, they have become partakers of the Divine nature: they are sons. Their appointment is mentioned; "inherit the kingdom prepared for you, from before the foundation of the world." Their name is "blessed," their nature is that of a child, their appointment is that of God's decree.

*Their doings,* their outward doings, these we want to speak a minute upon. They appear to have been distinguished among men for deeds of charity, and these were not in any way associated with ceremonies or outward observances. It is not said that they preached—they did so, some of them; it is not said that they prayed—they must have done so, or they would not have been spiritually alive. The actions which are selected as their type are actions of charity to the indigent and forlorn. Why these? I think, because *the general audience assembled around the throne would know how to appreciate this evidence of their newborn nature.* The King might think more of their prayers than of their alms, but the multitude would not. He speaks so as to gain the verdict of all assembled. Even their enemies could not object to his calling those blessed who had performed these actions; for if there be an action which wins for men the universal consent to their goodness, it is an action by which men would be served. Against this there is no law. I have never heard of a state in which there was a law against clothing the naked and feeding the hungry. Humanity at once, when its conscience is so seared that it cannot see its own sinfulness, yet detects the virtuousness of feeding the poor. Doubtless this is one reason why these actions were selected. And again, they may have been chosen as evidences of grace, because, *as actions, they are a wonderful means of separating between the hypocrite and the true Christian.* Dr. Gill has an idea, and perhaps he is right, that this is not a picture of the general judgment, but of the judgment of the professing church, and if so, it is all the more reasonable to conclude that these works of mercy are selected as the appropriate discerner between the hypocrite and the sincere. I fear that there are some of you high professors who could not stand the test. "Good praying people" they call you, but what do you give to the Lord? Your religion has not touched your pockets. This does not apply to some of you, for there are many here of whom I would venture to speak before the bar of God, that I know their substance to be consecrated to the Lord and his poor, and I have sometimes thought that beyond their means they have given both to the poor and to God's cause. But there are others of a very different disposition.

Now here I shall give you a little plain English talk which none can fail to understand. You may talk about your religion till you have worn your tongue out, and you may get others to believe you; and you may remain in the church twenty years, and nobody ever detect you in anything like an inconsistency; but, if it be in your power, and you do nothing to relieve the necessities of the poor members of Christ's body, you will be damned as surely as if you were drunkards or whoremongers. If you have no care for God's church this text applies to you, and will as surely sink you to the lowest hell as if you had been common blasphemers. That is very plain English, but it is the plain meaning of my text, and it is at my peril that I flinch from telling you of it. "I was an hungered, and you gave me"—what? Good advice; yes, but no meat. "I was thirsty, and you gave me"—what? A tract, and no drink. "I was naked, and you gave me"—what? Your good wishes, but no clothes. I was a stranger and—you pitied me, but—you took me not in. I was sick, you said you could recommend me a doctor, but you did not visit me. I was in prison, I, God's servant, a persecuted one, put in prison for Christ's sake, and you said I should be more cautious; but you did not stand by my side and take a share of the blame, and bear with me reproach for the truth's sake. You see this is a very terrible winnowing fan to some of you tightfisted ones whose main object is to get all you can and hold it fast, but it is a fan which frequently must be used. Whoever deceives you or spares you, by the grace of God, I will not, but will labor to be more bold than ever in denouncing sin. "Well," says one, "what are those to do who are so poor that they have nothing to give away?" My dear brother, do you notice how beautifully the text takes care of you? It hints that there are some who cannot give bread to the hungry, and clothes to the naked, but what about them? Why you see they are the persons spoken of as "my brethren," who receive the boon of kindness, so that this passage comforts the poor and by no means condemns them. Certain of us honestly give to the poor all we can spare, and then of course everybody comes to such; and when we say, "Really, I cannot give any more," somebody snarls and says, "Call yourself a Christian?" "Yes, I do, I should not call myself a Christian if I gave away other people's money; I should not call myself a Christian if I gave away what I have not got; I should call myself a thief, pretending to be charitable when I could not pay my debts." I have a very great pity indeed for those people who get into the bankruptcy court. I do not mean the debtors; I have seldom much sympathy with them. I have a good deal for the creditors who lose by having trusted dishonest people. If any man should say, "I will live beyond my means in order to get a good character," my dear brother, you begin wrong, that action is in itself wrong. What you have to give must be that which is your own. "But I shall have to pinch myself," says one, "if I do it." Well, pinch yourself! I do not think there is half the pleasure in doing good till you get to the pinching point. This remark of course applies only to those of us of moderate means, who can soon distribute our alms and get down to the pinch point. When you begin to feel, "Now, I must go without that; now I must curtail these in order to do more good." Oh! you cannot tell; it is then when you really can feel, "Now I have not given God merely the cheese parings and candle ends that I could not use, but I have really cut out for my Master a good piece of the loaf; I have not given him the old crusts that were getting moldy, but I have given him a piece of my own daily bread, and I am glad to do it, if I can show my love to Jesus Christ by denying myself." If you are doing this, if you are thus out of love to Jesus feeding the hungry, clothing the naked, I believe that these are put down as tests, because they are such blessed detectives between the hypocrites and the really godly people. When you read "for" here, you must not understand it to be that their reward is *because* of this, but that they are proved to be God's servants by this; and so, while they do not merit it because of these actions, yet these actions show that they were saved by grace, which is evidenced by the fact that Jesus Christ worked such and such works in them. If Christ does not work such things in you, you have no part in him; if you have not produced such works as these, you have not believed in Jesus. Now somebody says, "Then I intend to give to the poor in the future in order that I may have this reward." Ah, but you are very much mistaken if you do that.

The duke of Burgundy was waited upon by a poor man, a very loyal subject, who brought him a very large root which he had grown. He was a very poor man indeed, and every root he grew in his garden was of consequence to him; but merely as a loyal offering he brought to his prince the largest his little garden produced. The prince was so pleased with the man's evident loyalty and affection that he gave him a very large sum. The steward thought, "Well, I see this pays; this man has got fifty pounds for his large root, I think *I* shall make the duke a present." So he bought a horse and he reckoned that he should have in return ten times as much for it as it was worth, and he presented it with that view: the duke, like a wise man, quietly accepted the horse, and gave the greedy steward nothing. That was all. So you say, "Well, here is a Christian man, and he gets rewarded. He has been giving to the poor, helping the Lord's church, and see he is saved; the thing pays, I shall make a little investment." Yes, but you see the steward did not give the horse out of any idea of loyalty and kindness and love to the duke, but out of very great love to himself, and therefore had no return; and if you perform deeds of charity out of the idea of getting to heaven by them, why it is yourself that you are feeding, it is yourself that you are clothing; all your virtue is not virtue, it is rank selfishness, it smells strong of selfhood, and Christ will never accept it; you will never hear him say "thank you" for it. You served yourself, and no reward is due. You must first come to the Lord Jesus Christ, and look to him to save you; you will forever abjure all idea of doing anything to save yourself, and being saved, you will be able to give to the poor and so on without selfishness mixing with your motive, and you will get a reward of grace for the love token which you have given. It is necessary to believe in Christ in order to be capable of true virtue of the highest order. It is necessary to trust Jesus, and to be yourself fully saved, before there is any value in your feeding the hungry or clothing the naked. God give you grace to go to my Master wounded yonder, and to rest in the precious atonement which he has made for human sin; and when you have done that, being loved at such a rate, show that you love in return; being purchased so dearly, live for him that bought you; and among the actions by which you prove it, let these gleam and glisten like God-given jewels—the visiting of the sick, the comforting of the needy, the relieving of the distressed, and the helping of the weak. God accept these offerings as they come from gracious souls, and to him be praise evermore. Amen.

# The Great White Throne

---

Delivered on Sunday evening, August 12, 1866, at the Metropolitan Tabernacle, Newington. No. 710.

*And I saw a great white throne, and him that sat on it, from whose face the earth and the heaven fled away; and there was found no place for them.*
—REVELATION 20:11

Many of the visions which John saw are very obscure, and although a man who is assured of his own salvation may possibly be justified in spending his days in endeavoring to interpret them, yet I am sure of this, that it will not be a profitable task for unconverted persons. *They* have no time to spare for speculations, for they have not yet made sure of positive certainties. *They* need not dive into difficulties, for they have not yet laid a foundation of simplicities by faith in Christ Jesus. Better far to meditate upon the atonement than to be guessing at the little horn, and better far to know the Lord Jesus in his power to save than to fabricate an ingenious theory upon the number of the beast. But *this* particular vision is so instructive, so unattended by serious difficulties, that I may invite all here present to consider it, and the more so because it has to do with matters which concern our own eternal prospects. It may be, if God the Holy Spirit shall illuminate the eyes of our faith to look and see that "great white throne and him that sat upon it," that we may reap so much benefit from the sight as forever to make the arches of heaven ring with gratitude that we were brought in this world to look at the "great white throne," for by so doing we shall not be afraid to look upon it in the day when the Judge shall sit, and the quick and dead shall stand before him.

I shall, first, endeavor to explain what John saw; and then, in the second place, I shall try to set forth the effect which I think would be produced by this sight if the eyes of our faith should now be fixed thereon.

**1. First, then, I have to call your very earnest attention to *what John saw*.**

It was a scene of the last day, that wondrous day whose coming none can tell.

> *For, as a thief unheard, unseen, it steals*
> *Through night's dark shade.*

When the eagle-eyed seer of Patmos, being in the Spirit, looked aloft into the heavens, *he saw a throne,* from which I gather that there is a throne of moral government over the sons of men, and that he who sits upon it presides over all the inhabitants of this world. There is a throne whose dominion reaches from Adam in paradise down to "the last man," whoever he may be. We are not without a governor, lawgiver, and judge. This world is not left so that men may do in it as they will, without a legislator, without an avenger, without One to give reward or to inflict punishment. The sinner, in his blindness, looks, but he sees no throne; and therefore he cries, "I will live as I list, for there is none to call me to account"; but John, with illuminated eye, distinctly saw a throne, and a personal ruler upon it, who sat there to call his subjects to account. When our faith looks through the glass of revelation it sees a throne too. It were well for us if we felt more fully the influence of that ever-present throne. That "the Lord reigns" is true, believer, tonight, and true at all times. There is a throne whereon sits the King eternal, immortal, invisible; the world is governed by laws made and kept in force by an intelligent lawgiver. There is a moral governor. Men are accountable and will be brought to account at the last great day, when they shall all be either rewarded or punished. "I saw a great white throne." How this invests the actions of men with solemnity!

If we were left to do exactly as we willed without being called to account for it, it were wise even then to be virtuous, for rest assured it is best for ourselves that we should be good, and it is in itself malady enough to be evil. But we are not so left. There is a law laid down, to break which involves a penalty. There is a lawgiver who looks down and spies every action of man and who does not suffer one single word or deed to be omitted from his notebook. That governor is armed with power; he is soon coming to hold his assize, and every responsible agent upon the face of the earth must appear at his bar and receive, as we are told, "according to the deeds done in the body, whether they be good or whether they be evil." Let it, then, be gathered from the text that there is in very deed a personal and real moral governor of the world, an efficient and suitable ruler, not a mere name, not a myth, not an empty office, but a person who sits on the throne, who judges right, and who will carry out that judgment before long. Now, brethren and sisters, we know that this moral governor is God himself, who has an undisputed *right* to reign and rule. Some thrones have no right to be, and to revolt from them is patriotism; but the best lover of his race delights the most in the monarchy of heaven. Doubtless there are dynasties which are tyrannies, and governors who are despots; but none may dispute the right of God to sit upon the throne, or wish that another hand held the scepter. He created all, and shall he not judge all? He had a right, as Creator, to lay down his laws, and, as those laws are the very pattern of everything that is good and true, he had, therefore, because of this an eternal right to govern, in addition to the right which belonged to him as Creator. He is the Judge of all, who must do right from a necessity of his nature. Who else, then, should sit upon the throne, and who shall dare to claim to do so? He may cast down the gauntlet to all his creatures, and say, "I am God, and beside me there is none else;" if he reveals the thunder of his power, his creatures must silently own that he is Lord alone. None can venture to say that this throne is not founded upon right.

Moreover, there are some thrones on which the kings, however right, are deficient in *might,* but this is not the case with the King of kings. We constantly see little princes whose crowns fit their heads so ill that they cannot keep them on their brows; but our God has might invincible as well as right infallible. Who shall meet him in the battle? Shall the stubble defy the fire, or shall the wax make war with the flame? Jehovah can easily swallow up his enemies when they set themselves in battle array against him. "Behold he toucheth the hills, and they smoke; he looketh upon the mountains, and they tremble; he breaketh Leviathan in pieces in the depths of the sea. The winds are his chariots, and the tempests are his messengers. At his bidding there is day, and at his will night covereth the earth. Who shall stay his hand, or say unto him, 'What doest thou?'" His throne is founded in right and supported by might. You have justice and truth to settle it, but you have omnipotence and wisdom to be its guards, so that it cannot be moved.

In addition to this, his throne is one *from the power of which none can escape.* The sapphire throne of God, at this moment, is revealed in heaven, where adoring angels cast their crowns before it; and its power is felt on earth, where the works of creation praise the Lord. Even those who acknowledge not the divine government are compelled to feel it, for he does as he wills, not only among the angels in heaven, but among the inhabitants of this lower world. Hell feels the terror of that throne. Those chains of fire, those pangs unutterable, are the awful shadow of the throne of Deity; as God looks down upon the lost, the torment that flashes through their souls darts from his holiness, which cannot endure their sins. The influence of that throne, then, is found in every world where spirits dwell, and in the realms of inanimate nature it bears rule. Every leaf that fades in the trackless forest trembles at the Almighty's bidding, and every coral insect that dwells in the unfathomable depths of the sea feels and acknowledges the presence of the all-present King.

So, then, my brethren, if such is the throne which John saw, see how impossible it will be for you to escape from its judgment when the great day of assize shall be proclaimed, and the Judge shall issue his summons, bidding you appear. Where can the enemies of God flee? If up to heaven their high-flown impudence could carry them, his right hand of holiness would hurl them thence, or, if under hell's profoundest wave they dive, to seek a sheltering grave, his left hand would pluck them out of the fire, to expose them to the fiercer light of his countenance. Nowhere is there a refuge from the most High. The morning beams cannot convey the fugitive so swiftly as the almighty Pursuer could follow him; neither can the mysterious lightning flash, which annihilates time and space, journey so rapidly as to escape his far-reaching hand. "If I mount up to heaven, thou art there; if I make my bed in hell, thou art there." It was said of the Roman Empire under the Caesars that the whole world was only one great prison for Caesar, for if any man offended the emperor it was impossible for him to escape. If he crossed the Alps, could not Caesar find him out in Gaul? If he sought to hide himself in the Indies, even the swarthy monarchs there knew the power of the Roman arms, so that they would give no shelter to a man who had incurred imperial vengeance. And yet, perhaps, a fugitive from Rome might have prolonged his miserable life by hiding in the dens and caves of the earth. But O sinner, there is no hiding from God! The mountains cannot cover you from him, even if they would, neither can the rocks conceal you. See, then, at the very outset how this throne should awe our minds with terror. Founded in right, sustained by might, and universal in its dominion, look you and see the throne which John of old beheld.

This, however, is but the beginning of the vision. The text tells us that it was a "white throne," and I would call your attention to that. "I saw a great white throne." Why white? Does not this indicate its immaculate purity? There is no other white throne, I fear, to be found. The throne of our own happy land I believe to be as white and as pure as any throne might well be on earth, but there have been years, even in the annals of that throne, when it was stained with blood, and not many reigns back it was black with debauchery. Not always was it the throne of excellence and purity, and even now, though our throne possesses a lustrous purity, rare enough among earthly thrones, yet in the sight of God there must be in everything that is earthly something that is impure, and therefore the throne is not white to him. As for many other thrones that are still existing, we know that with them all is not white; this is neither the day nor the hour for us to call the princes to the bar of God, but there are some of them who will have much to answer for, because in their schemes of aggrandizement they took no account of the blood which would be shed, or of the rights which would be violated. Principle seldom moves the royal mind, but the knavish law of policy is the basis of kingcraft; a policy worthy of highwaymen and burglars, and some kings are little. On the continent of Europe, there are not a few thrones which I might describe as either black or crimson, as I think of the turpitude of the conduct of the monarch, or of the blood through which he has waded his way to dominion. But this is a great white throne, a throne of hallowed monarchy that is not stained with blood nor defiled with injustice.

Why, then, is it white for purity? Is it not because the King who sits on it is pure? Hark to the thrice-sacred hymn of the cherubic band and the seraphic choir, "Holy, holy, holy, Lord God of Sabaoth." Creatures who are perfectly spotless themselves unceasingly reverence and adore the yet superior holiness of the great King. He is too great to need to be unjust, and he is too good to be unkind. This King has done no wrong, and can do no wrong, but he is the only King of whom this can be said without fiction. He who sits on this white throne is himself the essence of holiness, justice, truth, and love. O fairest of all thrones! who would not be a willing subject of your peerless government?

Moreover, the throne is pure, because *the law the Judge dispenses is perfect*. There is no fault in the statute book of God. When the Lord shall come to judge the earth, there will be found no decree that bears too hardly upon any one of his creatures. "The statutes of the Lord are right"; they are true and righteous altogether. That book of the ten commands in which you find a summary of the divine will, who can improve it? Who can find anything in excess in it, or point out anything that is wanting? "The law of the Lord is perfect, converting the soul," and well may that be a white throne from which there emanates such a law. But you know that with a good law and a good lawgiver, yet sometimes the throne may make mistakes, and it may be stained by ignorance, if not by willful injustice. But the sentence which shall go forth from this great white throne, shall be so consistent with justice that even the condemned culprit himself must give his unwilling assent to it. "They stood speechless," it is said; speechless because they could neither bear the sentence nor in any way impugn it. It is a white throne, since never was a verdict delivered from it of which the culprit had a right to complain. Perhaps there are some here who view this as a matter of hope, but to ungodly persons it will be the very reverse. O sinner, if you had to be judged before an impure tribunal, you might, perhaps, escape; if the King were not holy, unholiness might, perhaps, go unpunished; if the law were not perfect, offenses might be condoned; or if the sentence were not just you might, through partiality, escape. But where everything is so pure and white,

> *Careless sinner,*
> *What will there become of thee?*

I have thought, too, that perhaps this throne is said to be a white throne to indicate that *it will be eminently conspicuous.* You will have noticed that a white object can be seen from a very great distance. You may have observed, perhaps, on the Welsh mountains, a white cottage far away, standing out conspicuously, for the Welsh like to make their cottages intensely white, so that though you would not have perceived it, had it been left of a stone color, you see it at once, for the bright whitewashed walls catch your eye. I suppose that a marksman would prefer a white object to aim at before almost any other color. And this great white throne will be so conspicuous that all the millions who were dead, but who shall rise at the sound of the last trumpet, shall all see it, nor shall it be possible for a single eye to close itself against the sight. We must see it; it shall be so striking a sight that none of us will be able to prevent its coming before us; "every eye *shall* see him."

Possibly it is called a white throne because of its being such a *convincing contrast to all the colors of this sinful human life.* There stand the crowd, and there is the great white throne. What can make them see their blackness more thoroughly than to stand there in contrast with the perfections of the law, and the Judge before whom they are standing? Perhaps that throne, all glistening, will reflect each man's character. As each unforgiven man shall look at that white throne, its dazzling whiteness will overcome him, and cover him with confusion and with terror when he sees his own defilement in contrast with it. "O God!" says he, "how can I bear to be judged by such a one as you are? I could face the judgment seat of my fellows, for I could see imperfections in my judges, but I cannot face you, you dread Supreme, for the awful whiteness of your throne, and the terrible splendor of your holiness utterly overcome me. Who am I, sinner as I am, that I should dare to stand before that great white throne?"

The next word that is used by way of adjective is "great." It was a *"great white throne."* You scarcely need me to tell you that it is called a great white throne because of the *greatness of him who sits upon it*. Speak of the greatness of Solomon? He was but a petty prince. Speak of the throne of the mogul or his celestial majesty of China, or of the thrones of Rome and Greece before which multitudes of beings assembled? They are nothing, mere representatives of associations of the grasshoppers of the world, who are as nothing in the sight of the Lord Jehovah. A throne filled by a mortal is but a shadow of dominion. This will be a great throne because on it will sit the great God of earth and heaven and hell, the King eternal, immortal, invisible, who shall judge the world in righteousness, and his people with equity. Brethren, you will see that this will be a "great white throne" when we remember *the culprits who will be brought before it*; not a handful of criminals, but millions upon millions, "multitudes, multitudes, in the Valley of Decision"; and these not all of the lesser sort, not serfs and slaves alone whose miserable bodies rested from their oppressors in the silent grave; but the great ones of the earth shall be there; not alone the downtrodden serf who toiled for nothing, and felt it sweet to die, but his tyrant master who fattened on his unrewarded toils shall be there; not alone the multitudes who marched to battle at their master's bidding, and who fell beneath the shot and the shell, but the emperors and kings who planned the conflict shall be there; crowned heads no greater than heads uncrowned. Men who were demigods among their fellows shall mix with their slaves, and be made as vile as they! What a marvelous procession! With what awe the imagination of it strikes the heart! What a pompous appearing! Aha! aha! you downtrodden multitudes, the great leveler has put you all upon a footing now! Death laid you in one equal grave, and now judgment finds you standing at one equal bar, to receive the sentence of one who fears no king, and dreads no tyrant, who has no respect of persons, but who deals justice alike to all. Can you picture the sight? Land and sea are covered with the living who once were dead. Hell is empty, and the grave has lost its victims! What a sight will that be! Xerxes on his throne with a million marching before him must have beheld a grand spectacle, but what will this be? No flaunting banner, but the ensigns of eternal majesty. No gaudy courtiers, but assembled angels! No sound of drum nor roar of culverin [cannon], but the blast of the archangel's trumpet, and the harping of ten thousand times ten thousand holy ones. There will be unrivaled splendor it is true, but not that of heraldry and war; mere tinsel and bauble shall have all departed, and in their place there shall be the splendor of the flashing lightning, and the deep bass of the thunder. Jesus the Man of sorrows, with all his angels with him shall descend, the pomp of heaven being revealed among the sons of men.

It will be a *great* white throne, because of *the matters that will be tried there*. It will be no mere quarrel about a suit in chancery or an estate in jeopardy. Our souls will have to be tried there; our future, not for an age, not for one single century, but forever and forever. Upon those balances shall hang heaven and hell; to the right shall be distributed triumph without end, to the left destruction and confusion without a pause, and the destiny of every man and woman shall be positively declared from that tremendous throne! Can you perceive the greatness of it? You must measure heaven; you must fathom hell, you must compass eternity, but until you can do this you cannot know the greatness of this *great* white throne; great, last of all, because throughout eternity there shall always be a looking back to the transactions of that day. That day shall be unto you, you saints, "the beginning of days," when he shall say, "Come, ye blessed of my Father." And that day shall be to you who perish the beginning of days too; just as that famous night of old in Egypt, when the firstborn were spared in every house where the lamb had shed its blood, was the first of days to Israel, but to Egypt the night when the firstborn felt the avenging angel's sword was a dread beginning of nights forever. Many a mother reckoned from that night when the destroyer came, and so shall you reckon throughout a dread eternity from the day when you see this great white throne.

Turn not away your eyes from the magnificent spectacle till you have seen the glorious Person mentioned in the words, "And him that sat on it." I wonder whether anything I have said has made you solemnly to think of the great day. I am afraid I cannot speak so as to get at your hearts, and if not I had better be silent; but do now for a moment think upon him who sat upon the great white throne. The most fitting one in all the world will sit upon that throne. It will be God, but hearken, it will also be man. "He shall judge the world by this man. Christ Jesus, according to my gospel," says the apostle. The Judge must needs be God. Who but God were fit to judge so many, and to judge so exactly? The throne is too great for any but for him of whom it is written, "Thy throne, O God, is forever and ever; a scepter of righteousness is thy scepter." Christ Jesus, the Son of God, will judge, and he will judge as man as well as God; and how fitting it is that it should be so! As man he knows our infirmities, he understands our hearts, and we cannot object to this, that our Judge should be himself like unto us. Who better could judge righteous judgment than one who is "bone of our bone and flesh of our flesh"? And then, there is this fitness about it; he is not only God and man, but he is *the* man, the man of men, of all men the most manly, the type and pattern of manhood.

He will be the test in his own person, for if a man be like Christ, that man is right, but if a man be otherwise than Christlike, that man deserves to be condemned. That wondrous Judge needs only look upon his own character to read the law, and to review his own actions to discern whether other men's actions be right or wrong. The thoughts of many hearts were revealed by Christ on earth, and that same Christ shall make an open exhibition of men at the last great day. He shall judge them, he shall discern their spirits, he shall find out the joints and the marrow of their being; the thoughts and intents of the heart he shall lay bare. Even you, believer, will pass the test before him; let no man deceive you with the delusion that you will not be judged: the sheep appeared before the great dividing Shepherd as well as the goats, those who used their talents were called to account as well as he who buried his pound, and the disciples themselves were warned that their idle words would bring them into judgment. Nor need you fear a public trial. Innocence courts the light. You are not saved by being allowed to be smuggled into heaven untested and unproved, but you will in the righteousness of Jesus pass the solemn test with joy. It may not be at the same moment as the wicked that the righteous shall be judged (I shall not contend for particulars), but I am clear that they will be judged, and that the blood and righteousness of Jesus are provided for this very cause, that they may find mercy of the Lord in *that* day. O sinner! It is far otherwise with you, for your ruin is sure when the testing time comes. There will be no witnesses needed to convict you, for the Judge knows all. The Christ whom you despised will judge you, the Savior whose mercy you trampled on, in the fountain of whose blood you would not wash, the despised and rejected of men—it is he who shall judge righteous judgment to you, and what will he say but this, "As for these mine enemies, who would not that I should reign over them, cut them in pieces before my eyes!"

**2. I want a few minutes—and I have but too few left—*to draw the inferences which flow from such a sight as this,* and so turn the vision to practical account.**

Believer in Christ, a word in your ear. Can you see the great white throne, and him that sits upon it? I think I see it now. Then, *let me search myself.* Whatever profession I may make, I shall have to face that great white throne. I have passed the elders; I have been approved by the pastor; I stand accepted by the church; but that great white throne is not passed yet. I have borne a reputable character among my fellow Christians; I have been asked to pray in public, and my prayers have been much admired, but I have not yet been weighed in the last balances, and what if I should be found wanting? Brother Christian, what about your private prayers? Can you live in neglect of the closet, and yet remember that your prayers will be tried before the great white throne? Is your Bible left unread in private? Is your religion nothing but a public show and sham? Remember the great white throne, for mere pretense will not pass there. Brother Christian, what about your heart and your treasure? Are you a mere money hunter? Do you live as others live? Is your delight in the fleeting present? Do you have dealings with the throne of heaven? Have you a stony heart toward divine things? Have you little love to Christ? Do you make an empty profession, and nothing more? Oh, think of that great white throne, that great white throne! Why, there are some of you, who, when I preach a stirring sermon, feel afraid to come again to hear me. Ah! but if you are afraid of my voice, how will you bear *his* voice who shall speak in tones of thunder? Do searching sermons seem to go through you like a blast of the north wind, chilling your very marrow and curdling your blood? Oh! but what must it be to stand before that dread tribunal? Are you doubting now? What will you be then? Can you not bear a little self-examination? How will you bear that God-examination? If the scales of earth tell you that you are wanting, what message will the scales of heaven give you? I do conjure you, fellow professors, speaking to you as I desire to speak now to my own heart, "Examine yourselves, whether you be in the faith; prove your own selves. Know you not your own selves, how that Jesus Christ is in you, except you be reprobates?"

Having spoken a word to the Christian, I should like to say to every one of you, in remembrance of this great white throne shun hypocrisy. Are you tempted to be baptized though you are not a believer, in order to please parents and friends? Beware of that great white throne, and consider how your insult to God will look at that great day! Are you persuaded to put on the cloak of religion because it will help your business, or make you seem respectable? Beware, you hypocrite, beware of that great white throne; for of all the terrors that shall come forth from it, there shall be none more severe than those which shall scathe the mere professor, who made a profession of religion for gain. If you must be damned, be damned anyhow sooner than as a hypocrite; for they deserve the deepest hell who for gain make a profession of godliness. The ruin of By-Ends and Hypocrisy will be just indeed. O you high-flying professors, whose wings are fastened on with wax, beware of the sun which will surely pour its heat upon you, for fearful will be your fall from so great a height!

But there are some of you who say, "I do not make any profession of religion." Still my text has a word to you. Still I want you to judge your actions by that last great day. O sir, how about that night of sin? "No," say you, "never mind it; bring it not to my remembrance." It shall be brought to your remembrance, and that deed of sin shall be published far wider than upon the housetops, gazetted to all the multitudes who have ever lived since the first man, and your infamy shall become a byword and a proverb among all created beings. What think you of this, you secret sinners? You lovers of wantonness and chambering? Ah! young man, you have commenced by filching, but you will go on to be a downright thief. It is known, sir, and "be sure your sin will find you out." Young woman, you have begun to dally with sin, and you think none has seen you, but the most mighty One has seen your acts and heard your words; there is no curtain between him and your sin. He sees you clearly, and what will you do with these sins of yours that you think have been concealed? "It was many years ago," you tell me. Yes, but though buried these many years to you, they are all alive to him, for everything is present to the all-seeing God; and your forgotten deeds shall one day stand out present to you also. My hearers, I conjure you do nothing which you would not do if you thought God saw you, for he does see you. Oh! look at your actions in the light of the judgment. Oh! that secret tippling of yours, how will that look when God reveals it? That private lust of yours which nobody knows of—how would you dare to do it if you recollected that God knows it? Young man, it is a secret, a fearful secret, and you would not whisper it in anyone's ear; but it shall be whispered, no, it shall be thundered out before the world! I pray you, friend, think of this. There is an observer who takes notes of all that we do, and will publish all to an assembled universe.

And as for us all, *are we ready to meet that last great day?* I had many things to say unto you, but I cannot keep you to say them now, lest you grow weary; but if tonight the trumpet should be sounded, what would be your state of mind? Suppose that now every ear in this place should be startled with a blast most loud and dread, and a voice were heard,

*Come to judgment,*
*Come to judgment, come away.*

Supposing some of you could hide in the vaults and in the foundations, would not many of you rush to the concealment? How few of us might go down these aisles walking steadily into the open air and saying, "I am not afraid of judgment, for 'there is therefore now no condemnation to them that are in Christ Jesus.'" Brethren and sisters, I hope there are some of us who could go gladly to that judgment seat, even if we had to traverse the jaws of death to reach it. I hope there are some of us who can sing in our hearts—

> *Bold shall I stand in that great day;*
> *For who aught to my charge shall lay?*
> *While, through thy blood, absolved I am*
> *From sin's tremendous curse and blame.*

It might put many of us much about to say that. It is easy to speak of full assurance, but, believe me, it is not quite so easy to have it in right down earnest in trying times. If some of you get the finger ache, your confidence oozes out at your joints, and if you have but a little sickness, you think, "Ah! it may be cholera, what shall I do?" Can you not bear to die, how then will you bear to live forever? Could you not look death in the face without a shudder, then how will you endure the judgment? Could you gaze upon death and feel that he is your friend and not your foe? Could you put a skull upon your dressing table and commune with it as your *memento mori*? Oh! it may well take the bravest of you to do this, and the only sure way is to come as we are to Jesus, with no righteousness of our own to trust to, but finding all in him. When William Carey was about to die, he ordered to have put upon his tombstone this verse—

> *A guilty, weak, and helpless worm,*
> *On Christ's kind arms I fall,*
> *He is my strength, my righteousness,*
> *My Jesus, and my all.*

I would like to wake up in eternity with such a verse as that in my mind, as I wish to go to sleep in this world with such a hope as that in my heart—

> *Nothing in my hand I bring,*
> *Simply to the cross I cling.*

Ah! I am talking about what some of us will know more of, perhaps, before this week is over. I am speaking now upon themes which you think are a long way off, but a moment may bring them near. A thousand years is a long time, but how soon it flies! One almost seems, in reading English history, to go back and shake hands with William the Conqueror; a few lives soon bring us even to the flood. You who are getting on to be forty years old, and especially you who are sixty or seventy, must feel how fast time flies. I only seem to preach a sermon one Sunday in time to get ready for the next. Time flies with such a whirl that no express train can overtake it, and even the lightning flash seems to lag behind it. We shall soon be at the great white throne; we shall soon be at the judgment bar of God. Oh! let us be making ready for it. Let us not live so much in this present, which is but a dream, an empty show, but let us live in the real, substantial future. Oh, that I could reach some heart here tonight! I have a notion that I am speaking to someone here who will not have another warning. I am sure that with such throngs as crowd here Sabbath after Sabbath, I never preach to the same congregation twice. There are always some here who are dead between one Sunday and another. Out of such masses as these it must be so according to the ordinary computation. Who among you will it be who will die this week? Oh! ponder the question well! Who among you will dwell with the devouring flames? Who among you will abide with everlasting burnings? If I knew you I would fain bedew you with tears. If I knew you who are to die this week, I would fain come and kneel down at your side, and conjure you to think of eternal things. But I do not know you, and therefore by the living God I do implore you all to fly to Jesus by faith. These are no trifles, sirs, are they? If they be, I am but a sorry trifler, and you may go your ways and laugh at me; but if they be true and real, it becomes me to be in earnest, and much more does it become you to be in earnest. "Prepare to meet your God!" He comes! Prepare now! "Now is the accepted time; now is the day of salvation!" The gates of mercy are not closed. Your sin is not unpardonable. You may yet find mercy. Christ invites you. His blood drops cry to you—

*Come and welcome,*
*Come and welcome, sinner come.*

Oh! may the Holy Spirit put life into these poor words of mine, and may the Lord help you to come now. The way to come, you know, is just to trust in Christ. It is all done when you trust in Christ, throw yourselves right on him, having nothing else to trust to. See now, my whole weight leans on the front of this platform. Should this rail give way, I fall. Lean on Christ just in that way.

*Venture on him, venture wholly,*
*Let no other trust intrude.*

If you can get a grip of the cross, and stand there beneath the crimson canopy of the atonement, God himself cannot smite you, and the last tremendous day shall dawn upon you with splendor and delight, and not with gloom and terror.

I must send you away, but not until all believers present have given you an invitation to return to the Lord Jesus. To do this we will sing the following verses—

*Return, O wanderer, to thy home.*
*Thy Father calls for thee;*
*No longer now an exile roam*
*In guilt and misery;*
*Return, return.*

*Return, O wanderer, to thy home,*
*'Tis Jesus calls for thee:*
*The Spirit and the bride say, Come;*
*Oh, now for refuge flee;*
*Return, return.*

*Return, O wanderer, to thy home,*
*'Tis madness to delay;*
*There are no pardons in the tomb,*
*And brief is mercy's day.*
*Return, return.*

# The Great Assize

Delivered on Lord's Day evening, August 25, 1872, at the Metropolitan Tabernacle, Newington. No. 1076.

*For we must all appear before the judgment seat of Christ; that everyone may receive the things done in his body, according to that he hath done, whether it be good or bad.* —2 Corinthians 5:10

This morning we preached concerning the resurrection of the dead, and it seems consistent with order to carry forward our thoughts this evening, to that which follows immediately after the resurrection, namely, the general judgment; for the dead rise on purpose that they may be judged in their bodies. The resurrection is the immediate prelude to the judgment. There is no need that I try to prove to you from Scripture that there will be a general judgment, for the Word of God abounds with proof passages. You have them in the Old Testament. You find David anticipating that great assize in the Psalms (especially in such as the forty-ninth and fiftieth, the ninety-sixth Psalm, and the three that follow it), for most assuredly the Lord comes: he comes to judge the earth in righteousness. Very solemnly and very tenderly does Solomon in the Ecclesiastes warn the young man, that, let him rejoice as he may and cheer his heart in the days of his youth, for all these things God will bring him into judgment; for God will judge every secret thing. Daniel in the night visions beholds the Son of man coming with the clouds of heaven and drawing near to the Ancient of Days; then he sits upon the throne of judgment and the nations are gathered before him. It was no new doctrine to the Jews; it was received and accepted by them as a most certain fact that there would be a day in which God would judge the earth in righteousness. The New Testament is very express. The twenty-fifth of Matthew, which we read to you just now, contains language, which could not possibly be more clear and definite, from the lips of the Savior himself. He is the faithful Witness and cannot lie. You are told that before him will be gathered all nations, and he shall divide them the one from the other, as the shepherd divides the sheep from the goats. Other passages there are in abundance, as, for instance, the one that is now before us, which is plain enough. Another we might quote is in the Second Epistle to the Thessalonians, the first chapter, from the seventh to the tenth verse. Let us read it, "And to you who are troubled rest with us, when the Lord Jesus shall be revealed from heaven with his mighty angels, in flaming fire taking vengeance on them that know not God, and that obey not the gospel of our Lord Jesus Christ: who shall be punished with everlasting destruction from the presence of the Lord, and from the glory of his power; when he shall come to be glorified in his saints, and to be admired in all them that believe (because our testimony among you was believed) in that day."

The book of the Revelation is very graphic in its depicting that last general judgment. Turn to the twentieth chapter, at the eleventh and twelfth verses. The seer of Patmos says, "And I saw a great white throne, and him that sat on it, from whose face the earth and the heaven fled away; and there was found no place for them. And I saw the dead, small and great, stand before God; and the books were opened: and another book was opened, which is the book of life: and the dead were judged out of those things which were written in the books, according to their works." Time would fail me to refer you to all the Scriptures. It is asserted over and over again by the Holy Spirit, whose word is truth, that there will be a judgment of the quick and of the dead.

Beside that direct testimony, it should be remembered there is a cogent argument that so it must needs be, from the very fact that God is just as the ruler over men. In all human governments there must be an assize held. Government cannot be conducted without its days of session and of trial, and, inasmuch as there is evidently sin and evil in this world, it might fairly be anticipated that there would be a time when God will go on circuit, and when he will call the prisoners before him, and the guilty shall receive their condemnation. Judge for yourselves: is this present state the conclusion of all things? If so, what evidence would you adduce of the divine justice, in the teeth of the fact that the best of men are often in this world the poorest and the most afflicted, while the worst of men acquire wealth, practice oppression, and receive homage from the crowd? Who are they that ride in the high places of the earth? Are they not those, great transgressors, who "wade through slaughter to a throne and shut the gates of mercy on mankind"? Where are the servants of God? They are in obscurity and suffering full often. Do they not sit like Job among the ashes, subjects of little pity, objects of much upbraiding? And where are the enemies of God? Do not many of them wear purple and fine linen and fare sumptuously every day? If there be no hereafter, then Dives has the best of it; and the selfish man who fears not God is, after all, the wisest of men and more to be commended than his fellows. But it cannot be so. Our common sense revolts against the thought. There must be another state in which these anomalies will all be rectified. "If in this life only we have hope in Christ, we are of all men the most miserable," says the apostle. The best of men were driven to the worst of straits in those persecuting times for being God's servants. How say you then, *Finis coronat opus*, the end crowns the work? That cannot be the final issue of life, or justice itself were frustrated. There must be a restitution for those who suffer unjustly: there must be a punishment for the wicked and the oppressor.

Not only may this be affirmed from a general sense of justice, but there is in the conscience of most men, if not of all, an assent to this fact. As an old Puritan says, "God holds a petty session in every man's conscience, which is the earnest of the assize which he will hold by and by; for almost all men judge themselves, and their conscience knows this to be wrong and that to be right. I say 'almost all,' for there seems to be in this generation a race of men who have so stultified their conscience that the spark appears to have gone out, and they put bitter for sweet and sweet for bitter. The lie they seem to approve, but the truth they do not recognize. But let conscience alone and do not stupify her, and you shall find her bearing witness that there is a Judge of all the earth who must do right." Now this is peculiarly the case when conscience is allowed full play. Men who are busy about their work or entertained with their pleasures often keep their consciences quiet. As John Bunyan puts it, they shut up Mr. Conscience; they blind his windows; they barricade his doors; and as for the great bell on the top of the house, which the old gentleman was inclined to ring, they cut the rope of it, so that he cannot get at it, for they do not wish him to disturb the town of Mansoul. But when death comes, it often happens that Mr. Conscience escapes from his prison house, and then, I warrant you, he will make such a din that there is not a sleeping head in all Mansoul. He will cry out and avenge himself for his constrained silence, and make the man know that there is a something within him not quite dead, which cries out still for justice, and that sin cannot go unchastised. There must be a judgment, then. Scripture asserts it, that would be enough: but by way of collateral evidence the natural order of things requires it; and conscience attests it.

Now we come to consider what our text says about the judgment. I pray you, brethren, if I should speak coldly tonight on this momentous truth, or fail to excite your attention and stir your deepest emotions, forgive me, sirs; and may God forgive me, for I shall have good reason to ask God's forgiveness, seeing that if ever a topic should arouse the preacher to a zeal for the honor of his Lord and for the welfare of his fellow creatures, and so make him doubly in earnest, it is this. But, then, permit me to say, that, if ever there was a theme quite independent of the speaker, which on its own account alone should command your thoughtfulness, it is that which I now bring before you. I feel no need of oratory or of speech well selected: the bare mention of the fact that such a judgment is impending, and will before long occur, might well hold you in breathless silence, still the very throbbings of your pulse, and choke the utterance of my lips. The certainty of it, the reality of it, the terrors that accompany it, the impossibility of escaping from it, all appeal to us now and demand our vigilance.

**1. Ask now, *who is it,* or *who are they that will have to appear before the throne of judgment?***

The answer is plain; it admits of no exemption: "We must *all* appear before the judgment seat of Christ." This is very decisive, if there were no other text. We must all appear; that is to say, every one of the human race. We must all appear. And that the godly will not be exempted from this appearance is very clear, for the apostle here is speaking to Christians. He says, "We walk by faith, not by sight. We are confident. We labor," and so on; and then he puts it, "We must all appear." So that, beyond all others, it is certain that all Christians must appear there. The text is quite conclusive upon that point. And if we had not that text, we have the passage in Matthew, which we have read, in which the sheep are summoned there as certainly as are the goats; and the passage in the Revelation, where all the dead are judged according to the things which are written in the books. They are all there. And if the objection should be raised, "We thought that the sins of the righteous being pardoned, and forever blotted out, they could never come into judgment," we have only to remind you, beloved, that if they are so pardoned and blotted out, as they undoubtedly are, the righteous have no reason to fear coming into judgment. They are the persons who covet the judgment, and will be able to stand there to receive a public acquittal from the mouth of the great Judge. Who among us wishes, as it were, to be smuggled into heaven unlawfully? Who desires to have it said by the damned in hell, "You were never tried, or else you might have been condemned as we were." No, brethren, we have a hope that we can stand the trial. The way of righteousness by Christ Jesus enables us to submit ourselves to the most tremendous tests which even that burning day can bring forth. We are not afraid to be put into the balances. We even desire that day when our faith in Jesus Christ is strong and firm; for we say, "Who is he that condemns?" We can challenge the day of judgment. Who is he that shall lay anything to our charge in that day, or at any other, since Christ has died and has risen again? It is needful that the righteous should be there that there may not be any partiality in the matter whatever; that the thing may be all clear and straight, and that the rewards of the righteous may be seen to be, though of grace, yet without any violation of the most rigorous justice. Dear brethren, what a day it will be for the righteous! For some of them were—perhaps some here present are—lying under some very terrible accusation of which they are perfectly guiltless. All will be cleared up then, and that will be one great blessing of that day. There will be a resurrection of reputations as well as of bodies. Men call the righteous, fools: then shall they shine forth as the sun in the kingdom of their Father. They hounded them to death, as not being fit to live. In early ages they laid to the Christians charges of the most terrible character, which I should count it shame to mention. But then they will all be clear; and those of whom the world was not worthy, who were driven and hunted about and made to dwell in the caves of the earth, they shall come forth as worthy ones, and the world shall know her true aristocracy, earth shall own her true nobility. The men whose names she cast out as evil shall then be held in great repute, for they shall stand out clear and transparent without spot or blemish. It is well that there should be a trial for the righteous, for the clearing of them, the vindication of them, and that it should be public, defying the cavil and criticism of all mankind.

"We must *all* appear." What a vast assembly, what a prodigious gathering, that of the entire human race! It struck me as I was meditating upon this subject, what would be the thoughts of Father Adam, as he stood there with Mother Eve and looked upon his offspring. It will be the first time in which he has ever had the opportunity of seeing all his children met together. What a sight will he then behold—far stretching, covering all the globe which they inhabit, enough not only to people all earth's plains, but crown her hilltops, and cover even the waves of the sea, so numberless must the human race have been, if all the generations that have ever lived, or shall ever live, shall at once rise from the dead! Oh, what a sight will that be! Is it too marvelous for our imagination to picture? Yet it is quite certain that the assemblage will be mustered, and the spectacle will be beheld. Everyone from before the flood, from the days of the patriarchs, from the times of David, from the Babylonian kingdom, all the legions of Assyria, all the hosts of Persia, all the phalanx of the Greeks, all the vast armies and legions of Rome, the barbarian, the Scythian, the bond, the free, men of every color and of every tongue—they shall all stand in that great day before the judgment seat of Christ. There come the kings—no greater than the men they call their slaves. There come the princes—but they have doffed their coronets, for they must stand like common flesh and blood. Here come the judges, to be judged themselves, and the advocates and barristers, needing an advocate on their own account. Here come those that thought themselves too good, and kept the street to themselves. There are the Pharisees, hustled by the publicans on either side and sunk down to the natural level with them. Mark the peasants rising from the soil; see the teeming myriads from outside the great cities streaming in, countless hosts such as no Alexander or Napoleon ever beheld! See how the servant is as great as his master! "Liberty, Equality, Fraternity" are now proclaimed. No kings, no princes, no nobles, can shelter themselves behind their order, assert a privilege or claim an immunity. Alike on one common level they stand together, to be tried before the last tremendous tribunal. There shall come the wicked of every sort. Proud Pharaoh shall be there; Sennacherib, the haughty; Herod, that would have slain the young child; Judas, that betrayed his Master; Demas, that sold him for gold; and Pilate, who would fain have washed his hands in innocence. There shall come the long list of infallibles, the whole line of popes, to receive their damnation at the Almighty's hands, and the priests that trod upon the necks of nations, and the tyrants that used the priests as their tools—they shall come to receive the thunderbolts of God which they so richly deserve. Oh, what a scene will it be! These little companies, which look to us so large when they are gathered together beneath this roof, how do they shrink into the drop of a bucket as compared with the ocean of life that shall swell around the throne at the last great judgment day. They shall all be there.

Now, the most important thought connected with this to me is that I shall be there; to you young men, that you will be there; to you, you aged of every sort, that you, *in propria persona*—each one shall be there. Are you rich? Your dainty dress shall be put off. Are you poor? Your rags shall not exempt you from attendance at that court. None shall say, "I am too obscure." You must come up from that hiding place. None shall say, "I am too public." You must come down from that pedestal. Everyone must be there. Note the word "we." "*We* must *all* appear."

And still further note the word "appear." "We must all *appear*." No disguise will be possible. You cannot come there dressed in masquerade of profession or attired in robes of state, but we must *appear*; we must be seen through, must be displayed, must be revealed; off will come your garments, and your spirit will be judged of God, not after appearance, but according to the inward heart. Oh, what a day that will be when every man shall see himself, and every man shall see his fellow, and the eyes of angels and the eyes of devils, and the eyes of God upon the throne, shall see us through and through. Let these thoughts dwell upon your minds, while you take this for the answer to our first inquiry, who is to be judged?

## 2. Our second question is, *who will be the Judge?*

"We must all appear before the judgment seat of Christ." That Christ should be appointed judge of all mankind is most proper and fitting. Our British law ordains that a man shall be tried by his peers, and there is justice in the statute. Now the Lord God will judge men, but at the same time it will be in the person of Jesus Christ the man. Men shall be judged by a man. He that was once judged by men shall judge men. Jesus knows what man should be; he has been under the law himself in deep humility, who is ordained to administer the law in high authority. He can hold the scales of justice evenly, for he has stood in man's place and borne and braved man's temptations; he therefore is the most fit judge that could be selected. I have sometimes heard and read sermons in which the preacher said that a Christian ought to rejoice that his Judge is his friend. There may be no impropriety intended, still it seems to me rather a questionable suggestion. I should not like to put it in that way myself; because any judge that was partial to his friends when he sat on the judgment seat would deserve to come off the seat immediately. As a judge I expect no favoritism from Christ. I expect when he sits there he will deal out evenhanded justice to all. I cannot see how it is right for any minister to hold it forth that we should find encouragement in the Judge being our friend. Friend or no friend, we shall go in for a fair trial every one of us, and Christ will not be a respecter of persons. Of him whom God has appointed to judge the world, it shall not be said when the assize is over that he winked at the crimes of some and extenuated them, while he searched out the faults of others and convicted them. He will be fair and upright throughout. He is our friend, I grant you, and he will be our friend and Savior forever; but, as a judge, we must keep to the thought, and believe and maintain it that he will be impartial to all the sons of men. You will have a fair trial, man. He that will judge you will not take sides against you. We have sometimes thought that men have been shielded from the punishment they deserved, because they were of a certain clerical profession, or because they occupied a certain official position. A poor laborer who kills his wife shall be hanged, but when another man of superior station does the like deed of violence, and stains his hands with the blood of her whom he had vowed to love and cherish, the capital sentence shall not be executed upon him. Everywhere we see in the world that with the best intentions justice somehow or other does squint a little. Even in this country there is just the slightest possible turning of the scale, and God grant that may be cured before long. I do not think it is intentional, and I hope the nation will not long have to complain about it. There ought to be the same justice for the poorest beggar that crawls into a casual ward, as for his lordship that owns the broadest acres in all England. Before the law, at least, all men ought to stand equal. So shall it be with the Judge of all the earth. *Fiat justitia, ruat caelum.* Christ will by all means hold the scales even. You shall have a fair trial and a full trial too. There shall be no concealment of anything in your favor, and no keeping back of anything against you. No witnesses shall be borne across the sea to keep them out of the way. They shall all be there, and all testimony shall be there, and all that is wanted to condemn or to acquit shall be produced in full court at that trial, and hence it will be a final trial. From that court there will be no appeal. If Christ says, "Cursed!" cursed must they be forever. If Christ says, "Blessed!" blessed shall they be forever. Well, this is what we have to expect then, to stand before the throne of the man Christ Jesus the Son of God, and there to be judged.

### 3. Now the third point is, *what will be the rule of judgment?*

The text says "that everyone may receive the things done in his body according to that he hath done, whether it be good or bad." Then it would appear that our *actions* will be taken in evidence at the last. Not our profession, not our boastings, but our actions will be taken in evidence at the last, and every man shall receive according to what he has done in the body. That implies that everything done by us in this body will be known. It is all recorded; it will be all brought to light. Hence, in that day every secret sin will be published. What was done in the chamber, what was hidden by the darkness, shall be published as upon the housetop—every secret thing. With great care you have concealed it, most dexterously you have covered it up; but it shall be brought out to your own astonishment to form a part of your judgment. There, hypocritical actions as well as secret sins will be laid bare. The Pharisee who devoured the widow's house and made a long prayer will find that widow's house brought against him and the long prayer too, for the long prayer will then be understood as having been a long lie against God from beginning to end. Oh, how fine we can make some things look with the aid of paint and varnish and gilt; but at the last day off will come the varnish and veneer, and the true metal, the real substance, will then be seen.

When it is said that everything that is done in the body will be brought up as evidence against us or for us, remember this includes every omission as well as every commission; for that which is not done that ought to have been done is as greatly sinful as the doing of that which ought not to be done. Did not you notice when we were reading that twenty-fifth chapter of Matthew, how those on the left hand were condemned, not for what they did, but for what they did not do: "I was an hungered, and you gave me no meat: I was thirsty, and you gave me no drink." Where would some of you stand, according to this rule, who have lived in neglect of holiness, and neglect of faith, and neglect of repentance, before all your days? Consider yourselves, I pray you.

Recollect, too, that all our words will be brought up. For every idle word that man shall speak he will have to give an account. And all our thoughts too, for these lie at the bottom of our actions and give the true color to them good or bad. Our motives, our heart sins, especially, our hatred of Christ, our neglect of the gospel, our unbelief—all of these shall be read aloud and published unreservedly. "Well," says one, "who then can be saved?" Ah! indeed, who then can be saved! Let me tell you who. There will come forward those who have believed in Jesus, and albeit they have many sins to which they might well plead guilty, they will be able to say, "Great God, you did provide for us a substitute, and you did say that if we would accept him he should be a substitute for us and take our sins upon himself, and we did accept him and our sins were laid on him, and we have now no sins; they have been transferred from us to the great Savior, substitute and sacrifice." And in that day there will be none who can put in a demurrer to that plea: it will hold good; for God has said, "Whosoever believeth on Christ Jesus shall never be condemned." Then will the actions of the righteous, the gracious actions, be brought forth to prove that they had faith. For that faith which never evidences itself by good works is a dead faith and a faith that will never save a soul. Now, if the dying thief were brought up, he would say, "My sins were laid on Jesus." "Yes, but how about your good works? You must have some evidence of your faith," Satan might reply. Then would the recording angel say, "The dying thief said to his fellow thief who was dying with him, 'Wherefore are you railing?' In his last moments he did what he could: he rebuked the thief that was dying with him and made a good confession of his Lord. There was the evidence of the sincerity of his faith." Dear hearer, will there be any evidence of the sincerity of your faith? If your faith has no evidence before the Lord, what will you do? Suppose you thought you had a faith and went on drinking. Suppose you did as I know some have done here, go straight from this place into the public house? Or suppose you joined the Christian church and remained a drunkard? Yes, and women have done that also as well as men. Suppose you professed to have faith in Christ and yet cheated in your weights and measures and common dealings? Do you think that God will never require these things at your hands? O sirs, if you be no better than other men in your conduct, you *are* no better than other men in your character, and you will stand no better than other men in the judgment day. If your actions are not superior to theirs, you may profess what you will about your faith, but you are deceived, and, as deceivers, you will be discovered at the last great day. If grace does not make us differ from other men, it is not the grace which God gives his elect. We are not perfect, but all God's saints keep their eyes on the great standard of perfection, and, with strong desire, aim to walk worthy of their high calling of God and to bring forth works which prove that they love God; and if we have not these signs following faith, or if they are not put in as evidence for us, at the last great day we shall not be able to prove our faith. O you who have no faith in Christ, no faith in Jesus the substitute; that terrible negative, that treacherous unbelief of yours, will be a condemning sin against you! It will be proof positive that you hated God; for a man must hate God indeed who will spurn his counsels, give no heed to his reproof, scorn his grace, and dare the vengeance of him who points out the way of escape and the path that leads to life. He that will not be saved by God's mercy proves that he hates the God of mercy. If God gives his own Son to die and men will not trust in his Son, will not have him as their Savior, that one sin, if they had no other, would at once prove that they were enemies of God and black at heart. But if your faith be in Jesus, if you love Jesus, if your heart goes out to Jesus, if your life be influenced by Jesus, if you make him your example as well as your Savior, there will be evidence—you cannot see it, but there will be evidence—in your favor. For notice those gracious things, when the evidence was brought, and Christ said, "I was an hungered, and ye gave me meat—thirsty, and ye gave me drink," they said, "O Lord, we never knew this." Should any man stand up here and say, "I have plenty of evidence to prove my faith," I should reply, "Hold your tongue, sir! Hold your tongue! I am afraid you have no faith at all, or you would not be talking about your evidence." But if you are saying, "Oh, I am afraid I have not the evidence that will stand me in good stead at the last," yet if all the while you have been feeding the hungry, and clothing the naked, and doing all you can for Christ, I would tell you not to be afraid. The Master will find witnesses to say, "That man relieved me when I was in poverty. He knew I was one of Christ's and he came and helped me." And another will come and say (perhaps it will be an angel), "I saw him when he was alone in his chamber and heard him pray for his enemies." And the Lord will say, "I read his heart when I saw how he put up with rebuke, and slander, and persecution, and would not make any answer for my sake. He did it all as evidence that my grace was in his heart." You will not have to fetch up the witnesses: the Judge will call them, for he knows all about your case; and as he calls up the witnesses, you will be surprised to find how even the ungodly will be obliged to consent to the just salvation of the righteous. Oh, how the secret deeds and the true heart sincerity of the righteous, when thus unveiled, will make devils bite their tongues in wrath to think that there was so much of grace given to the sons of men, with which to defeat persecution, to overcome temptation, and to follow on in obedience to the Lord. Oh yes, the deeds, the deeds, the deeds of men—not their prating, not their profession, not their talk, but their deeds (though nobody shall be saved by the merits of his deeds)—their deeds shall be the evidence of their grace, or their deeds shall be the evidence of their unbelief; and so, by their works shall they stand before the Lord, or by their works shall they be condemned as evidence and nothing more.

4. Now the last point is this: *What is the object of this judgment?*

Will sentence of acquittal and condemnation be given, and then the whole thing be over? Far from it. The judgment is with a view to the thereafter—"That every man may receive the things done in his body." The Lord will grant unto his people an abundant reward for all that they have done. Not that they deserve any reward, but that God first gave them grace to do good works, then took their good works as evidence of a renewed heart, and then gave them a reward for what they had done. Oh, what a bliss it will be to hear it said, "Well done, good and faithful servant"—to you that have worked for Christ when nobody knew it, to find that Christ took stock of it all—to you that served the Lord under misrepresentation, to find that the Lord Jesus cleared the chaff away from the wheat, and knew that you were one of his precious ones. For him, then, to say, "Enter into the joy of thy Lord," oh, what a bliss will it be to you.

But to the ungodly how terrible. They are to receive the things that they have done; that is to say, the punishment due—not every man alike, but the greater sinner the greater doom; to the man who sinned against light a greater damnation than to the man who had not the same light—Sodom and Gomorrah their place, Tyre and Sidon their place, and then to Capernaum and Bethsaida their place of more intolerable torment, because they had the gospel and rejected it—so the Lord himself tells us. And the punishment will not only be meted out in proportion to the transgression, but it will be a development of the evil actions done in the evil consequences to be endured, as every man shall eat the fruit of his own ways. Sin, after the natural order, ripens into sorrow. This is not a blind fate, but it is the operation of a divine law, wise and invariable. Oh, how dreadful it will be for the malicious man to have forever to gnaw his own envious heart, to find his malice come home to him, as birds come home to roost, to hoot for forever in his own soul; for the lustful man to feel lust burning in every vein, which he can never gratify; for the drunkard to have a thirst, which not even a drop of water can allay; for the glutton who has fared sumptuously every day to be in hunger perpetually; and the soul that has been wrathful to be forever wrathful, with the fire of wrath forever burning like a volcano in his soul; and the rebel against God forever a rebel, cursing God whom he cannot touch, and finding his curses come back upon himself. There is no punishment worse than for a man who is sinfully disposed to gratify his lusts, to satiate his bad propensities, and to multiply and fatten his vices. Only let men grow into what they would be, and then see what they would be like! Take away the policemen in some parts of London, and give the people plenty of money, and let them do just as they like. Last Saturday, it may be, there were half a dozen broken heads, and wives and children were in one general skirmish. Keep those people together: let their vigor continue unimpaired by age or decay, while they keep on developing their characters. Why, they would be worse than a herd of tigers. Let them give way to their rage and anger, with nothing to check their passions; let miserly, greedy people forever go on with their greed. It makes them miserable here, but let these things be indulged in forever, and what worse hell do you want? Oh, sin is hell and holiness is heaven. Men will receive the things done in their body. If God has made them love him, they shall go on to love him; if God has made them trust him, they shall go on to trust in him; if God has made them to be like Christ, they shall go on to be like Christ, and they shall receive the things done in their body as a reward; but if a man has lived in sin, "he that is filthy shall be filthy still"; he that has been unbelieving shall be unbelieving still. This, then, shall be the worm that never dies, and the fire which never shall be quenched, to which shall be added the wrath of God forever and forever. Oh, that we may have grace every one of us to flee to Christ! There is our only safety. Simple faith in Jesus is the basis for the character which will evidence at last that you are chosen of God. A simple belief in the merit of the Lord Jesus, worked in us by the Holy Ghost, is the rocky foundation upon which shall be built up, by the same divine hands, the character which shall evidence that the kingdom was prepared for us from before the foundations of the world. God work in us such a character, for Christ's sake. Amen.

# Jesus Admired in Them That Believe

—∞—

Delivered on Lord's Day morning, June 1, 1879, at the Metropolitan Tabernacle, Newington. No. 1477.

*When he shall come to be glorified in his saints, and to be admired in all them that believe (because our testimony among you was believed) in that day.*
—2 Thessalonians 1:10

What a difference between the first and second comings of our Lord! When he shall come a second time it will be to be glorified and admired, but when he came the first time it was to be despised and rejected of men. He comes a second time to reign with unexampled splendor, but the first time he came to die in circumstances of shame and sorrow. Lift up your eyes, you sons of light, and anticipate the change, which will be as great for you as for your Lord; for now you are hidden even as he was hidden, and misunderstood even as he was misunderstood when he walked among the sons of men. "We know that, when he shall appear, we shall be like him; for we shall see him as he is." His manifestation will be our manifestation, and in the day in which he is revealed in glory then shall his saints be glorified with him.

Observe that our Lord is spoken of as coming in his glory, and as at the same time taking vengeance in flaming fire on them that know not God, and that obey not the gospel. This is a note of great terror to all those who are ignorant of God, and wickedly unbelieving concerning his Christ. Let them take heed, for the Lord will gain glory by the overthrow of his enemies, and those who would not bow before him cheerfully shall be compelled to bow before him abjectly: they shall crouch at his feet, they should lick the dust in terror, and at the glance of his eyes they shall utterly wither away, as it is written, they "shall be punished with everlasting destruction from the presence of the Lord, and from the glory of his power." But this is not the main object for which Christ will come, nor is this the matter in which he finds his chief glory, for, observe, he does this as it were by the way, when he comes for another purpose. To destroy the wicked is a matter of necessity in which his spirit takes no delight, for he does this, according to the text, not so much when he comes to do it as when he shall come with another object, namely, "to be glorified in his saints, and to be admired in them that believe."

The crowning honor of Christ will be seen in his people, and this is the design with which he will return to this earth in the latter days, that he may be illustrious in his saints and exceedingly magnified in them. Even now his saints glorify him. When they walk in holiness they do, as it were, reflect his light; their holy deeds are beams from him who is the Sun of righteousness. When they believe in him they also glorify him, for there is no grace which pays lowlier homage at the throne of Jesus than the grace of faith whereby we trust him, and so confess him to be our all in all. We do glorify our gracious Lord, but, beloved brethren, we must all confess that we do not this as we could desire, for, alas, too often we dishonor him, and grieve his Holy Spirit. By our want of zeal and by our many sins we are guilty of discrediting his gospel and dishonoring his name. Happy, happy, happy day when this shall no more be possible, when we shall be rid of the inward corruption which now works itself into outward sin, and shall never dishonor Christ again, but shall shine with a clear, pure radiance, like the moon on the Passover night, when it looks the sun full in the face, and then shines upon the earth at her best. Today we are like vessels on the wheel, but half fashioned, yet even now somewhat of his divine skill is seen in us as his handiwork. Still the unformed clay is in part seen, and much remains to be done; how much more of the great Potter's creating wisdom and sanctifying power will be displayed when we shall be the perfect products of his hand! In the bud and germ our new nature brings honor to its Author; it will do far more when its perfection manifests the Finisher. Then shall Jesus be glorified and admired in every one of us when the days of the new creation are ended and God shall usher in the eternal Sabbath by pronouncing his grace work to be very good.

This morning, as God shall help me, I shall speak first of *the special glorification of Christ here intended*: and, second, I shall conclude the sermon by calling your attention to *the special considerations which this grand truth suggests*.

## 1. Let us consider carefully *the special glorification here intended.*

And the first point to note is *the time*. The text says, "When he shall come to be glorified in his saints." The full glorification of Christ in his saints will be when he shall come a second time, according to the sure word of prophecy. He is glorified in them now, for he says, "All mine are thine, and thine are mine; and I am glorified in them"; but as yet that glory is perceptible to himself rather than to the outer world. The lamps are being trimmed, they will shine before long. These are the days of preparation before that Sabbath which is in an infinite sense a high day. As it was said of Esther, that for so many months she prepared herself with myrrh and sweet odors before she entered the king's palace, to be espoused of him, even so are we now being purified and made ready for that august day when the perfected church shall be presented unto Christ as a bride unto her husband. John says of her that she shall be "prepared as a bride adorned for her husband." This is our night, wherein we must watch, but behold the morning comes, a morning without clouds, and then shall we walk in a sevenfold light because our well beloved has come. That second advent of his will be his revelation: he was under a cloud here, and men perceived him not, save only a few who beheld his glory; but when he comes a second time all veils will be removed and every eye shall see the glory of his countenance. For this he waits and his church waits with him. We know not when the set time shall arrive, but every hour is bringing it nearer to us, therefore let us stand with loins girded, awaiting it.

Note, second, *in whom* this glorification of Christ is to be found. The text does not say he will be glorified "by" his saints, but "*in* his saints." There is a shade of difference, yes, more than a shade, between the two terms. We endeavor to glorify him now by our actions, but then he will be glorified in our own persons, and character, and condition. He is glorified *by* what we do, but he is at the last to be glorified in what we are. Who are these in whom Jesus is to be glorified and admired? They are spoken of under two descriptions: "in his saints," and "in all them that believe."

In "his saints" first. All those in whom Christ will be glorified are described as holy ones or saints: men and women who have been sanctified, and made pure, whose gracious lives show that they have been under the teaching of the Holy Spirit, whose obedient actions prove that they are disciples of a holy master, even of him who was "holy, harmless, undefiled, and separate from sinners." But, inasmuch as these saints are also said to be believers, I gather that the holiness which will honor Christ at last is a holiness based on faith in him, a holiness of which this was the root, that they first trusted in Christ, and then, being saved, they loved their Lord and obeyed him. Their faith worked by love and purified their souls, and so cleansed their lives. It is an inner as well as an outer purity, arising out of the living and operative principle of faith. If any think that they can attain to holiness apart from faith in Christ, they are as much mistaken as he who should hope to reap a harvest without casting seed into the furrows. Faith is the bulb, and saintship is the delightfully fragrant flower which comes of it when planted in the soil of a renewed heart. Beware, I pray you, of any pretense to a holiness arising out of yourselves, and maintained by the energy of your own unaided wills; as well look to gather grapes of thorns or figs of thistles. True saintship must spring from confidence in the Savior of sinners, and if it does not it is lacking in the first elements of truth. How can that be a perfect character which finds its basis in self-esteem? How could Christ be glorified by saints who refuse to trust in him?

I would call your attention once again to the second description, "All them that believe." This is enlarged by the hint that they are believers in a certain testimony, according to the bracketed sentence—"because our testimony among you was believed." Now, the testimony of the apostles was concerning Christ. They saw him in the body, and they bore witness that he was "God manifest in the flesh"; they saw his holy life, and they bore witness to it; they saw his death of grief, and they witnessed that "God was in Christ reconciling the world unto himself"; they saw him risen from the dead, and they said, "We are witnesses of his resurrection"; they saw him rise into heaven, and they bore witness that God had taken him up to his right hand. Now, all that believe this witness are saved. "If thou shalt confess with thy mouth the Lord Jesus, and shalt believe in thine heart that God hath raised him from the dead, thou shalt be saved." All who with a simple faith come and cast themselves upon the incarnate God, living and dying for men, and ever sitting at the right hand of God to make intercession for them, these are the people in whom Christ will be glorified and admired at the last great day. But inasmuch as they are first said to be saints, be it never forgotten that this faith must be a living faith, a faith which produces a hatred of sin, a faith which renews the character and shapes the life after the noble model of Christ, thus turning sinners into saints. The two descriptions must not be violently rent asunder; you must not say that the favored people are sanctified without remembering that they are justified by faith, nor may you say that they are justified by faith without remembering that without holiness no man shall see the Lord, and that at the last the people in whom Christ will be admired will be those holy ones who were saved by faith in him.

So far, then, we see our way, but now a question arises: *by whom* will Christ be thus glorified and admired? He shines in his people, but who will see the glory? I answer first, that his people will see it. Every saint will glorify Christ in himself, and admire Christ in himself. He will say, "What a wonder that such a poor creature as I am should be thus perfected! How glorious is my Lord, who has worked this miracle upon me!" Surely our consciousness of having been cleansed and made holy will cause us to fulfill those words of John Berridge which we sang just now—

> *He cheers them with eternal smile,*
> *They sing hosannas all the while;*

*Or, overwhelm'd with rapture sweet,*
*Sink down adoring at his feet.*

This I know, that when I personally enter heaven I shall forever admire and adore the everlasting love which brought me there. Yes, we will all glorify and admire our Savior for what he has worked in us by his infinite grace.

The saints will also admire Christ in one another. As I shall see you and you shall see your brethren and sisters in Christ all perfect, you will be filled with wonderment and gratitude and delight. You will be free from all envy there, and therefore you will rejoice in all the beauty of your fellow saints: their heaven will be a heaven to you, and what a multitude of heavens you will have as you will joy in the joy of all the redeemed! We shall as much admire the Lord's handiwork in others as in ourselves, and shall each one praise him for saving all the rest. You will see your Lord in all your brethren, and this will make you praise and adore him world without end with a perpetual amazement of ever-growing delight.

But that will not be all. Besides the blood bought and ransomed of Christ there will be on that great day of his coming all the holy angels to stand by and look on and wonder. They marveled much when first he stooped from heaven to earth, and they desired to look into those things, which then were a mystery to them. But when they shall see their beloved Prince come back with ten thousand times ten thousand of the ransomed at his feet, all of them made perfect by having washed their robes and made them white in his blood, how the principalities and powers will admire him in every one of his redeemed! How they will praise that conquering arm which has brought home all these spoils from the war! How will the hosts of heaven shout his praises as they see him lead all these captives captive with a new captivity, in chains of love, joyfully gracing his triumph and showing forth the completeness of his victory!

We do not know what other races of innocent creatures there may be but I think it is no stretch of imagination to believe that, as this world is only one speck in the creation of God, there may be millions of other races in the countless worlds around us, and all these may be invited to behold the wonders of redeeming love as manifested in the saints in the day of the Lord. I seem to see these unfallen intelligences encompassing the saints as a cloud of witnesses, and in rapt vision beholding in them the love and grace of the redeeming Lord. What songs! What shouts shall rise from all these to the praise of the ever-blessed God! What an orchestra of praise will the universe become! From star to star the holy hymn shall roll, till all space shall ring out the hosannas of wondering spirits. "The Wonderful, the Counselor, the mighty God, the everlasting Father, the Prince of peace" shall have brought home all the men wondered at, and they with himself shall be the wonder of eternity.

Then shall Satan and his defeated legions, and the lost spirits of ungodly men, bite their lips with envy and rage, and tremble at the majesty of Jesus in that day. By their confessed defeat and manifest despair, they shall glorify him in his people, in whom they have been utterly overthrown. They shall see that there is not one lost whom he redeemed by blood, not one snatched away of all the sheep his Father gave him, not one warrior enlisted beneath his banner fallen in the day of battle, but all more than conquerors through him that loved them. What despair shall seize upon diabolic spirits as they discover their entire defeat! Defeated in men who were once their slaves! Poor dupes whom they could so easily beguile by their craftiness, defeated even in these! Jesus, triumphant by taking the lambs from between the lion's jaws, and rescuing his feeble sheep from their power, will utterly put them to shame in his redeemed. With what anguish will they sink into the hell prepared for them, because now they hear with anger all earth and heaven and every star ringing with the shout, "Hallelujah, Hallelujah, Hallelujah, for the Lord God omnipotent reigns, and the Lamb hath conquered by his blood."

You see then that there are enough spectators to magnify Christ in his saints; and so, fourthly, let us inquire *in what degree* will the Lord Jesus be glorified? Our answer is, it will be to the very highest degree. He shall come to be glorified in his saints to the utmost, for this is clear from the words, "to be admired." When our translation was made, the word "admired" had to ordinary Englishmen a stronger flavor of wonder than it has to us now. We often speak of admiring a thing in the softer sense of loving it, but the real meaning of the English word, and of the Greek also, is *wonder*: our Lord will be wondered at in all them that believe. Those who look upon the saints will feel a sudden wonderment of sacred delight; they will be startled with the surprising glory of the Lord's work in them; "We thought he would do great things, but this! This surpasses conception!" Every saint will be a wonder to himself. "I thought my bliss would be great, but not like this!" All his brethren will be a wonder to the perfected believer. He will say, "I thought the saints would be perfect, but I never imagined such a transfiguration of excessive glory would be put upon each of them. I could not have imagined my Lord to be so good and gracious." The angels in heaven will say that they never anticipated such deeds of grace: they did know that he had undertaken a great work, but they did not know that he would do so much for his people and in his people. The firstborn sons of light, used to great marvels from of old, will be entranced with a new wonder as they see the handiwork of Emmanuel's free grace and dying love. The men who once despised the saints, who called them canting hypocrites and trampled on them, and perhaps slew them, the kings and princes of the earth who sold the righteous for a pair of shoes, what will they say when they see the least of the Savior's followers become a prince of more illustrious rank than the great ones of the earth, and Christ shining out in every one of these favored beings? For their uplifting Jesus will be wondered at by those who once despised both him and them.

My next point leads us into the very bowels of the subject; *in what respects will Christ be glorified and wondered at?* I cannot expect to tell you one tenth part of it. I am only going to give you a little sample of what this must mean; exhaustive expositions were quite impossible to me. I think with regard to his saints that Jesus will be glorified and wondered at on account of their number—"a number that no man can number." John was a great arithmetician, and he managed to count up to 144,000 of all the tribes of the children of Israel; but that was only a representative number for the Jewish church: as for the church of God, comprehending the Gentile nations, he gave up all idea of computation, and confessed that it is "a number which no man can number." When he heard them sing he says, "I heard a voice like the voice of many waters and like great thunder." There were so many of them that their song was like the Mediterranean sea lashed to fury by a tempest, no, not one great sea in uproar, but ocean upon ocean, the Atlantic and the Pacific piled upon each other, and the Arctic upon these, and other oceans upon these, layers of oceans, all thundering out their mightiest roar: and such will be the song of the redeemed, for the crowds which swell the matchless hymn will be beyond all reckoning. Behold, and see, you who laughed at his kingdom, see how the little one has become a thousand: Now look you, you foes of Christ, who saw the handful of corn on the top of the mountains; see how the fruit thereof does shake like Lebanon, and they of the city do flourish like grass of the earth. Who can reckon the drops of the dew or the sands on the seashore? When they have counted these then shall they not have guessed at the multitude of the redeemed that Christ shall bring to glory. And all this harvest from one grain of wheat, which except it had fallen into the ground and died would have remained alone! What said the Word? "If it die, it shall bring forth much fruit." Is not the prophecy fulfilled? O beloved, what a harvest from the lone Man of Nazareth! What fruit from that glorious man—the branch! Men esteemed him stricken, smitten of God, and afflicted; and they made nothing of him, and yet there sprang of him (and he as good as dead) these multitudes which are many as the stars of heaven. Is he not glorified and wondered at in them? The day shall declare it without fail.

But there is quality as well as quantity. He is admired in his saints because they are every one of them proofs of his power to save from evil. My eye can hardly bear, even though it be but in imagination, to gaze upon the glittering ranks of the white-robed ones, where each one outshines the sun, and they are all as if a sevenfold midday had clothed them. Yet all these, as I look at them, tell me, "We have washed our robes, for they were once defiled. We have made them white, but this whiteness is caused by the blood of the Lamb." These were heirs of wrath even as others, these were dead in trespasses and sins; all these like sheep had gone astray and turned every one to his own way; but look at them and see how he has saved them, washed them, cleansed them, perfected them! His power and grace are seen in all of them. If your eye will pause here and there, you will discover some that were supremely stubborn, whose neck was as an iron sinew, and yet he conquered them by love. Some were densely ignorant, but he opened their blind eyes; some grossly infected with the leprosy of lust, but he healed them; some under Satan's most terrible power, but he cast the devil out of them. Oh, how he will be glorified in special cases! In you drunkard made into a saint, in you blasphemer turned into a loving disciple, in you persecutor who breathed out threatening taught to sing everlastingly a hymn of praise! He will be exceedingly glorified in such. Brethren, beloved in the Lord, in each one of us there was some special difficulty as to our salvation, some impossibility which was possible with God, though it would have been forever impossible with us.

Remember, also, that all those saints made perfect would have been in hell had it not been for the Son's atoning sacrifice. This they will remember the more vividly, because they will see other men condemned for the sins with which they also were once polluted. The crash of vengeance upon the ungodly will make the saints magnify the Lord the more as they see themselves delivered. They will each feel—

> *Oh, were it not for grace divine,*
> *That fate so dreadful had been mine.*

In each one the memory of the horrible pit from which they were drawn and the miry clay out of which they were uplifted shall make their Savior more glorified and wondered at.

Perhaps the chief point in which Christ will be glorified will be—the absolute perfection of all the saints. They shall then be "without spot or wrinkle or any such thing." We have not experienced what perfection is, and therefore we can hardly conceive it; our thoughts themselves are too sinful for us to get a full idea of what absolute perfection must be; but, dear brethren, we shall have no sin left in us, for they are "without fault before the throne of God," and we shall have no remaining propensity to sin. There shall be no bias in the will toward that which is evil, but it shall be fixed forever upon that which is good. The affections will never be wanton again, they will be chaste for Christ. The understanding will never make mistakes. You shall never put bitter for sweet, nor sweet for bitter; you shall be "perfect, even as your Father which is in heaven is perfect": and truly, brethren, he who works this in us will be a wonder. Christ will be admired and adored because of this grand result. O mighty Master, with what strange moral alchemy did you work to turn that morose dispositioned man into a mass of love! How did you work to lift that selfish mammonite up from his hoarded gains to make him find his gain in you? How did you overcome that proud spirit, that fickle spirit, that lazy spirit, that lustful spirit—how did you contrive to take all these away? How did you extirpate the very roots of sin, and every little rootlet of sin, out of your redeemed, so that not a tiny fiber can be found? "The sins of Jacob shall be sought for and they shall not be found, yea, they shall not be, saith the Lord." Neither the guilt of sin nor the propensity to sin—both shall be gone, and Christ shall have done it, and he will be "glorified in his saints, and admired in them that believe."

This is but the beginning, however. There will be seen in every saint, in that last wondrous day, the wisdom and power and love of Christ in having brought them through all the trials of the way. He kept their faith alive when else it would have died out; he sustained them under trials when else they would have fainted; he held them fast in their integrity when temptation solicited them, and they had almost slipped with their feet. Yes, he sustained some of them in prison, and on the rack, and at the stake, and held them faithful still! One might hardly wish to be a martyr, but I reckon that the martyrs will be the admiration of us all, or rather Christ will be admired in them. However they could bear such pain as some of them did endure for Christ's sake none of us can guess, except that we know that Christ was in them suffering in his members. Eternally will Jesus be wondered at in them as all intelligent spirits shall see how he upheld them, so that neither tribulation nor distress nor nakedness nor famine nor sword could separate them from his love. These are the men that wandered about in sheepskins and goatskins, destitute, afflicted, tormented, of whom the world was not worthy, but now they stand arrayed as kings and priests in surpassing glory forever. Verily, their Lord shall be admired in them. Say you not so?

Recollect, dear friends, that we shall see in that day how the blessed Christ, as "Head over all things to his church," has ruled every providence to the sanctification of his people—how the dark days begat showers which made the plants of the Lord to grow, how the fierce sun which threatened to scorch them to the root, filled them with warmth of love divine and ripened their choice fruit. What a tale the saints will have to tell of how that which threatened to damp the fire of grace made it burn more mightily, how the stone which threatened to kill their faith was turned into bread for them, how the rod and staff of the good Shepherd was ever with them to bring them safely home. I have sometimes thought that if I get into heaven by the skin of my teeth I will sit down on the glory shore and bless forever him who, on a board, or on a broken piece of the ship, brought my soul safe to land; and surely they who obtain an abundant entrance, coming into the fair havens, like a ship in full sail, without danger of shipwreck, will have to praise the Lord that they thus came into the blessed port of peace: in each case the Lord will be specially glorified and admired.

I cannot stop over this, but I must beg you to notice that as a king is glorious in his regalia, so will Christ put on his saints as his personal splendor in that day when he shall make up his jewels. It is with Christ as it was with that noble Roman matron, who when she called at her friends' houses and saw their trinkets, asked them to come next day to her house, and she would exhibit her jewels. They expected to see ruby, and pearl, and diamond, but she called in her two boys, and said, "These are my jewels." Even so will Jesus, instead of emerald and amethyst and onyx and topaz, exhibit his saints. "These are my choice treasures," says he, "in whom I will be glorified." Solomon surely was never more full of glory than when he had finished the temple, when all the tribes came together to see the noble structure, and confessed it to be "beautiful for situation, the joy of the whole earth." But what will be the glory of Christ when all the living stones shall be put into their places and his church shall have her windows of agates and her gates of carbuncle, and all her borders of precious stones. Then, indeed, will he be glorified, when the twelve foundations of his new Jerusalem shall be courses of stones most precious, the like of which was never seen.

Now, inasmuch as my text lays special stress upon *believing*, I invite you just for a minute to consider how as believers as well as saints the saved ones will glorify their Lord.

First, it will be wonderful that there should be so many brought to faith in him: men with no God, and men with many gods, men steeped in ignorance, and men puffed up with carnal wisdom, great men and poor men, all brought to believe in the one Redeemer and praise him for his great salvation. Will he not be glorified in their common faith? It will magnify him that these will all be saved by faith, and not by their own merits. Not one among them will boast that he was saved by his own good works, but all of them will rejoice to have been saved by that blessedly simple way of "believe and live," saved by sovereign grace through the atoning blood, looked to by the tearful eye of simple faith. This, too, shall make Jesus glorious, that all of them, weak as they were, were made strong by faith; all of them personally unfit for battle were yet made triumphant in conflict because by faith they overcame through the blood of the Lamb. All of them shall be there to show that their faith was honored, that Christ was faithful to his promise, and never allowed them to believe in vain. All of them standing in heavenly places, saved by faith, will ascribe every particle of the glory to the Lord Jesus only—

> *I ask them whence their victory came?*
> *They, with united breath,*
> *Ascribe their conquest to the Lamb,*
> *Their triumph to his death.*

They believed and were saved, but faith takes no credit to itself; it is a self-denying grace, and puts the crown upon the head of Christ, and therefore is it written that he will be glorified in his saints, and he will also be admired in all them that believe.

I have scarcely skirted the subject even now, and time is failing me. I want you to reflect that Jesus will be glorified in the risen bodies of all his saints. Now, in heaven, they are pure spirits, but when he shall come they shall be clothed again. Poor body, you must sleep awhile, but what you shall be at your awaking does not yet appear. You are now the shriveled seed, but there is a flower to come of you which shall be lovely beyond all thought. Though sown in weakness, this body shall be raised in power; though sown in corruption, it shall be raised in incorruption. Weakness, weariness, pain, and death will be banished forever; infirmity and deformity will be all unknown. The Lord will raise up our bodies to be like unto his glorious body. Oh, what a prospect lies before us! Let us remember that this blessed resurrection will come to us because he rose, for there must be a resurrection to the members because the Head has risen. Oh, the charm of being a risen man perfect in body, soul, and spirit! All that charm will be due to Christ, and therefore he will be admired in us.

Then let us think of the absolute perfection of the church as to numbers: all who have believed in him will be with him in glory. The text says, he will be "admired in *all* them that believe." Now, if some of those who believe perished he would not be admired in them, but they will all be there, the little ones as well as the great ones. You will be there, you poor feeble folk who when you say, "Lord, I believe," are obliged to add, "help you mine unbelief." He shall be admired in all believers without a single exception, and peradventure there shall be more wonder at the going to heaven of the weak believers than at the stronger ones. Mr. Greatheart, when he comes there, will owe his victories to his Master and lay his laurels at his feet; but fainting Feeble-Mind, and limping Ready-to-Halt with his crutches, and trembling Little-Faith, when they enter into rest will make heaven ring with notes of even greater admiration that such poor creeping worms of the earth should win the day by mighty grace. Suppose that one of them should be missing at last! Stop the harps! Silence the songs! No beginning to be merry while one child is shut out! I am quite certain if as a family we were going to sing our evening hymn of joy and thankfulness, if mother said, "Where is the little mite? Where is the last one of the family?" there would be a pause. If we had to say—she is lost, there would be no singing and no resting till she was found. It is the glory of Jesus that as a shepherd he has lost none of his flock, as the Captain of salvation he has brought many sons to glory, and has lost none, and hence he is admired, not in some that believe, nor yet in all but one, but he is "admired in *all* them that believe."

Does not this delight you, you who are weak and trembling, that he will be admired in you? There is little to admire in you at present, as you penitently confess; but since Christ is in you now, and will be more fully manifested in you, there will before long be much to admire. May you partake in the excellence of our divine Lord and be conformed to his likeness that he may be seen in you and glorified in you.

Another point of admiration will be the eternal safety of all his believing people. There they are safe from fear of harm. You dogs of hell, you howled at their heels and hoped to devour them; but, lo, they are clean escaped from you! What must it be to be lifted above gunshot of the enemy, where no more watch shall need to be kept, for even the roar of the satanic artillery cannot be heard? O glorious Christ, to bring them all to such a state of safety, you are indeed to be wondered at forever.

Moreover, all the saints will be so honored, so happy, and so like their Lord that themselves and everything about them will be themes for never-ending admiration. You may have seen a room hung round with mirrors, and when you stood in the midst you were reflected from every point: you were seen here, and seen there, and there again, and there again, and so every part of you was reflected; just such is heaven, Jesus is the center, and all his saints like mirrors reflect his glory. Is he human? So are they! Is he the Son of God? So are they sons of God! Is he perfect? So are they! Is he exalted? So are they! Is he a prophet? So are they, making known unto principalities and powers the manifold wisdom of God. Is he a priest? So are they! Is he a King? So are they, for he has made us priests and kings unto God, and we shall reign forever and ever. Look where you will along the ranks of the redeemed, this one thing shall be seen, the glory of Christ Jesus, even to surprise and wonder.

**2. I have no time to make those *suggestions* with which I intended to have finished, and so I will just tell you what they would have been.**

First, the text suggests that the principal subject for self-examination with us all should be—Am I a saint? Am I holy? Am I a believer in Christ? Yes or no, for on that yes or no must hang your glorification of Christ, or your banishment from his presence.

The next thing is—observe the small value of human opinion. When Christ was here, the world reckoned him to be a nobody, and while his people are here they must expect to be judged in the same way. What do worldlings know about it? How soon will their judgment be reversed! When our Lord shall appear even those who sneered will be compelled to admire. When they shall see the glory of Christ in every one of his people, awestricken, they will have nothing to say against us; no, not even the false tongue of malicious slander shall dare to hiss out a serpent word in that day. Never mind them, then; put up with reproach which shall so soon be silenced.

The next suggestion is a great encouragement to inquirers who are seeking Christ; for I put it to you, you great sinners, if Jesus is to be glorified in saved sinners, would he not be glorified indeed if he saved you? If he were ever to save such a rebel as you have been, would it not be the astonishment of eternity? I mean you who are known in the village as Wicked Jack or known as a common swearer—what if my Master were to make a saint of you? Bad raw material! Yet suppose he transformed you into a precious jewel and made you to be as holy as God is holy, what would you say of him? "Say of him," say you, "I would praise him world without end." Yes, and you shall do so if you will come and trust him. Put your trust in him. The Lord help you to do so at once, and he shall be admired even in you forever and ever.

Our text gives an exhortation to believers also. Will Jesus Christ be honored and glorified in all the saints? Then let us think well of them all and love them all. Some dear children of God have uncomely bodies, or they are blind or deformed or maimed; and many of these have scanty purses, and it may be the church knows most of them as coming for alms: moreover, they have little knowledge, little power to please, and they are uncouth in manners and belong to what are called the lowest ranks of society: do not, therefore, despise them, for one day our Lord will be glorified in them. How he will be admired in yonder poor bedridden woman when she rises from the workhouse to sing hallelujah to God and the Lamb among the brightest of the shining ones. Why, I think the pain, the poverty, the weakness, and the sorrow of saints below will greatly glorify the Captain of their salvation as they tell how grace helped them to bear their burdens and to rejoice under their afflictions.

Lastly, brethren, this text ought to encourage all of you who love Jesus to go on talking about him to others and bearing your testimony for his name. You see how the apostle Paul has inserted a few words by way of parenthesis. Draw the words out of the brackets, and take them home, "because our testimony among you was believed." Do you see those crowds of idolatrous heathen, and do you see those hosts of saved ones before the throne? What is the medium which linked the two characters? By what visible means did the sinners become saints? Do you see that insignificant-looking man with weak eyes? That man whose bodily presence is weak and whose speech is contemptible? Do you not see his bodkin and needle case? He has been making and mending tents, for he is only a tentmaker. Now, those bright spirits which shine like suns, flashing forth Christ's glory, were made thus bright through the addresses and prayers of that tentmaker. The Thessalonians were heathens plunged in sin, and this poor tentmaker came in among them and told them of Jesus Christ and his gospel; his testimony was believed; that belief changed the lives of his hearers and made them holy, and they being renewed came at length to be perfectly holy, and there they are, and Jesus Christ is glorified in them. Beloved, will it not be a delightful thing throughout eternity to contemplate that you went into your Sunday school class this afternoon, and you were afraid you could not say much, but you talked about Jesus Christ with a tear in your eye, and you brought a dear girl to believe in his saving name through your testimony. In years to come that girl will be among those that shine out to the glory of Christ forever. Or you will get away this evening, perhaps, to talk in a lodging house to some of those poor, despised tramps; you will go and tell one of those poor vagrants, or one of the fallen women, the story of your Lord's love and blood, and the poor broken heart will catch at the gracious word, and come to Jesus, and then a heavenly character will be begun, and another jewel secured for the Redeemer's diadem. I think you will admire his crown all the more because, as you see certain stones sparkling in it, you will say, "Blessed be his name forever: he helped me to dive into the sea and find that pearl for him," and now it adorns his sacred brow. Now, get at it, all of you! You that are doing nothing for Jesus, be ashamed of yourselves, and ask him to work in you that you may begin to work for him, and unto God shall be the glory, forever and ever. Amen and amen.

# The Ascension and the Second Advent Practically Considered

❦

Delivered on Lord's Day morning, December 28, 1884, at the Metropolitan Tabernacle, Newington. No. 1817.

> *And while they looked steadfastly toward heaven as he went up, behold, two men stood by them in white apparel; which also said, "Ye men of Galilee, why stand ye gazing up into heaven? this same Jesus, which is taken up from you into heaven, shall so come in like manner as ye have seen him go into heaven."*
> —Acts 1:10–11

Four great events shine out brightly in our Savior's story. All Christian minds delight to dwell upon his birth, his death, his resurrection, and his ascension. These make four rounds in that ladder of light, the foot of which is upon the earth, but the top whereof reaches to heaven. We could not afford to dispense with any one of those four events, nor would it be profitable for us to forget, or to underestimate the value of any one of them. That the Son of God was born of a woman creates in us the intense delight of a brotherhood springing out of a common humanity. That Jesus once suffered unto the death for our sins, and thereby made a full atonement for us, is the rest and life of our spirits. The manger and the cross together are divine seals of love. That the Lord Jesus rose again from the dead is the warrant of our justification, and also a transcendently delightful assurance of the resurrection of all his people, and of their eternal life in him. Has he not said, "Because I live ye shall live also"? The resurrection of Christ is the morning star of our future glory. Equally delightful is the remembrance of his ascension. No song is sweeter than this—"Thou hast ascended on high; thou hast led captivity captive, thou hast received gifts for men, yea, for the rebellious also, that the Lord God might dwell among them."

Each one of those four events points to another, and they all lead up to it: the fifth link in the golden chain is our Lord's second and most glorious advent. Nothing is mentioned between his ascent and his descent. True, a rich history comes between; but it lies in a valley between two stupendous mountains: we step from alp to alp as we journey in meditation from the ascension to the second advent. I say that each of the previous four events points to it. Had he not come a first time in humiliation, born under the law, he could not have come a second time in amazing glory "without a sin offering unto salvation." Because he died once we rejoice that he died no more, death has no more dominion over him, and therefore he comes to destroy that last enemy whom he has already conquered. It is our joy, as we think of our Redeemer as risen, to feel that in consequence of his rising the trump of the archangel shall assuredly sound for the awaking of all his slumbering people, when the Lord himself shall descend from heaven with a shout. As for his ascension, he could not a second time descend if he had not first ascended; but having perfumed heaven with his presence, and prepared a place for his people, we may fitly expect that he will come again and receive us unto himself, that where he is there we may be also. I want you, therefore, as in contemplation you pass with joyful footsteps over these four grand events, as your faith leaps from his birth to his death, and from his resurrection to his ascension, to be looking forward, and even hastening unto this crowning fact of our Lord's history; for before long he shall so come in like manner as he was seen go up into heaven.

This morning, in our meditation, we will start from the ascension; and if I had sufficient imagination I should like to picture our Lord and the eleven walking up the side of Olivet, communing as they went, a happy company, with a solemn awe upon them, but with an intense joy in having fellowship with each other. Each disciple was glad to think that his dear Lord and Master who had been crucified was now among them, not only alive but surrounded with a mysterious safety and glory which none could disturb. The enemy was as still as a stone; not a dog moved his tongue; his bitterest foes made no sign during the days of our Lord's afterlife below. The company moved onward peacefully toward Bethany—Bethany which they all knew and loved. The Savior seemed drawn there at the time of his ascension, even as men's minds return to old and well-loved scenes when they are about to depart out of this world. His happiest moments on earth had been spent beneath the roof where lived Mary and Martha and their brother Lazarus. Perhaps it was best for the disciples that he should leave them at that place where he had been most hospitably entertained, to show that he departed in peace and not in anger. There they had seen Lazarus raised from the dead by him who was now to be taken up from them: the memory of the triumphant past would help the tried faith of the present. There they had heard the voice saying, "Loose him, and let him go," and there they might fitly see their Lord loosed from all bonds of earthly gravitation that he might go to his Father and their Father. The memories of the place might help to calm their minds and arouse their spirits to that fullness of joy which ought to attend the glorifying of their Lord.

But they have come to a standstill, having reached the brow of the hill. The Savior stands conspicuously in the center of the group, and, following upon most instructive discourse, he pronounces a blessing upon them. He lifts his pierced hands, and while he is lifting them and is pronouncing words of love, he begins to rise from the earth. He has risen above them all to their astonishment! In a moment he has passed beyond the olives, which seem with their silvery sheen to be lit up by his milder radiance. While the disciples are looking, the Lord has ascended into midair, and speedily he has risen to the regions of the clouds. They stand spellbound with astonishment, and suddenly a bright cloud, like a chariot of God, bears him away. That cloud conceals him from mortal gaze. Though we have known Christ after the flesh, now after the flesh know we him no more. They are riveted to the spot, very naturally so: they linger long in the place, they stand with streaming eyes, wonder struck, still looking upward.

It is not the Lord's will that they should long remain inactive; their reverie is interrupted. They might have stood there till wonder saddened into fear. As it was, they remained long enough; for the angel's words may be accurately rendered, "Why have you stood, gazing up into heaven?"

Their lengthened gaze needed to be interrupted, and, therefore, two shining ones, such as aforetime met the women at the sepulcher, are sent to them. These messengers of God appear in human form that they may not alarm them, and in white raiment as if to remind them that all was bright and joyous; and these white-robed ministers stood with them as if they would willingly join their company. As no one of the eleven would break silence, the men in white raiment commenced the discourse. Addressing them in the usual celestial style, they asked a question which contained its own answer, and then went on to tell their message. As they had once said to the women, "Why seek ye the living among the dead? He is not here, but is risen"; so did they now say, "Ye men of Galilee, why stand ye gazing up into heaven? this same Jesus, which is taken up from you into heaven, shall so come in like manner as ye have seen him go into heaven." The angels showed their knowledge of them by calling them "men of Galilee," and reminded them that they were yet upon earth by recalling their place of birth. Brought back to their senses, their reverie over, the apostles at once gird up their loins for active service; they do not need twice telling, but hasten to Jerusalem. The vision of angels has singularly enough brought them back into the world of actual life again, and they obey the command, "Tarry ye at Jerusalem." They seem to say, the taking up of our Master is not a thing to weep about: he has gone to his throne and to his glory, and he said it was expedient for us that he should go away. He will now send us the promise of the Father; we scarcely know what it will be like, but let us, in obedience to his will, make the best of our way to the place where he bade us await the gift of power. Do you not see them going down the side of Olivet, taking that Sabbath-day's journey into the cruel and wicked city without a thought of fear; having no dread of the bloodthirsty crew who slew their Lord, but happy in the memory of their Lord's exaltation and in the expectation of a wonderful display of his power? They held fellowship of the most delightful kind with one another, and anon entered into the upper room, where in protracted prayer and communion they waited for the promise of the Father. You see I have no imagination: I have barely mentioned the incidents in the simplest language. Yet try and realize the scene, for it will be helpful so to do, since our Lord Jesus is to come in like manner as the disciples saw him go up into heaven.

My first business this morning will be to consider *the gentle chiding* administered by the shining ones: "Ye men of Galilee, why stand ye gazing up unto heaven?" Second, *the cheering description* of our Lord which the white-robed messengers used, "This same Jesus"; and then, third, *the practical truth* which they taught, "This same Jesus, which is taken up from you into heaven, shall so come in like manner as ye have seen him go into heaven."

## 1. First, then, here is *a gentle chiding*.

It is not sharply uttered by men dressed in black who use harsh speech, and upbraid the servants of God severely for what was rather a mistake than a fault. No; the language is strengthening, yet tender: the fashion of a question allows them rather to reprove themselves than to be reproved; and the tone is that of brotherly love and affectionate concern.

Notice, that *what these saintly men were doing seems at first sight to be very right*. I think, if Jesus were among us now we would fix our eyes upon him, and never withdraw them. He is altogether lovely, and it would seem wicked to yield our eyesight to any inferior object so long as he was to be seen. When he ascended up into heaven, it was the duty of his friends to look upon him. It can never be wrong to look up; we are often bidden to do so, and it is even a holy saying of the psalmist, "I will direct my prayer unto thee, and will look up"; and, again, "I will lift up mine eyes unto the hills, from whence cometh my help." If it be right to look up into heaven, it must be still more right to look up while Jesus rises to the place of his glory. Surely it had been wrong if they had looked anywhere else; it was due to the Lamb of God that they should behold him as long as eyes could follow him. He is the Sun: where should eyes be turned but to his light? He is the King; and where should courtiers within the palace gate turn their eyes but to their King as he ascends to his throne? The truth is, there was nothing wrong in their looking up into heaven; but they went a little further than looking; they stood "gazing." A little excess in right may be faulty. It may be wise to look, but foolish to gaze. There is a very thin partition sometimes between that which is commendable and that which is censurable. There is a golden mean which it is not easy to keep. The exact path of right is often as narrow as a razor's edge, and he must be wise that does not err either on the right hand or on the left. "Look" is ever the right word. Why, it is "Look unto me, and be saved." Look, yes, look steadfastly and intently: be your posture that of one "looking unto Jesus," always throughout life. But there is a gazing which is not commendable, when the look becomes not that of reverent worship, but of an overweening curiosity, when there mingles with the desire to know what should be known, a prying into that which it is for God's glory to conceal. Brethren, it is of little use to look up into an empty heaven. If Christ himself be not visible in heaven, then in vain do we gaze, since there is nothing for a saintly eye to see. When the person of Jesus was gone out of the azure vault above them, and the cloud had effectually concealed him, why should they continue to gaze when God himself had drawn the curtain? If infinite wisdom had withdrawn the object upon which they desired to gaze, what would their gazing be but a sort of reflection upon the wisdom which had removed their Lord? Yet it did seem very right. Thus certain things that you and I may do may appear right, and yet we may need to be scolded out of them into something better: they may be right in themselves, but not appropriate for the occasion, not seasonable, nor expedient. They may be right up to a point, and then may touch the boundary of excess. A steadfast gaze into heaven may be to a devout soul a high order of worship, but if this filled up much of our working time, it might become the idlest form of folly.

Yet I cannot help adding that *it was very natural*. I do not wonder that the whole eleven stood gazing up, for if I had been there I am sure I should have done the same. How struck they must have been with the ascent of the Master out of their midst! You would be amazed if someone from among our own number now began to ascend into heaven! Would you not? Our Lord did not gradually melt away from sight as a phantom, or dissolve into thin air as a mere apparition: the Savior did not disappear in that way at all, but he rose, and they saw that it was his very self that was so rising. His own body, the materialism in which he had veiled himself, actually, distinctly, and literally, rose to heaven before their eyes. I repeat, the Lord did not dissolve, and disappear like a vision of the night, but he evidently rose till the cloud intervened so that they could see him no more. I think I should have stood looking to the very place where his cloudy chariot had been. I know it would be idle to continue so to do, but our hearts often urge us on to acts which we could not justify logically. Hearts are not to be argued with. Sometimes you stand by a grave where one is buried whom you dearly loved: you go there often to weep. You cannot help it, the place is precious to you; yet you could not prove that you do any good by your visits, perhaps you even injure yourself thereby, and deserve to be gently scolded with the question "why?" It may be the most natural thing in the world, and yet it may not be a wise thing. The Lord allows us to do that which is innocently natural, but he will not have us carry it too far; for then it might foster an evil nature. Hence he sends an interrupting messenger: not an angel with a sword, or even a rod; but he sends some man in white raiment—I mean one who is both cheerful and holy, and he, by his conduct or his words, suggests to us the question, "Why stand you here gazing?" *Cui bono?* What will be the benefit? What will it avail? Thus our understanding being called into action, and we being men of thought, we answer to ourselves, "This will not do. We must not stand gazing here forever," and therefore we arouse ourselves to get back to the Jerusalem of practical life, where in the power of God we hope to do service for our Master.

Notice, then, that the disciples were doing that which seemed to be right and what was evidently very natural, but that it is very easy to carry the apparently right and the absolutely natural too far. Let us take heed to ourselves, and often ask our hearts "why?"

For, third, notice that what they *did was not after all justifiable upon strict reason.* While Christ was going up it was proper that they should adoringly look at him. He might almost have said, "If you see me when I am taken up, a double portion of my spirit shall rest upon you." They did well to look where he led the way. But when he was gone, still to remain gazing was an act which they could not exactly explain to themselves and could not justify to others. Put the question thus: "What purpose will be fulfilled by your continuing to gaze into the sky? He is gone, it is absolutely certain that he is gone. He is taken up, and God himself has manifestly concealed all trace of him by bidding yonder cloud sail in between him and you. Why gaze you still? He told you, 'I go unto my Father.' Why stand and gaze?" We may under the influence of great love act unwisely. I remember well seeing the action of a woman whose only son was emigrating to a distant colony. I stood in the station, and I noticed her many tears and her frequent embraces of her boy; but the train came up and he entered the carriage. After the train had passed beyond the station, she was foolish enough to break away from friends who sought to detain her; she ran along the platform, leaped down upon the railroad and pursued the flying train. It was natural, but it had been better left undone. What was the use of it? We had better abstain from acts which serve no practical purpose; for in this life we have neither time nor strength to waste in fruitless action. The disciples would be wise to cease gazing, for nobody would be benefited by it, and they would not themselves be blessed. What is the use of gazing when there is nothing to see? Well, then, did the angels ask, "Why stand ye gazing up into heaven?"

Again, put another question: what precept were they obeying when they stood gazing up into heaven? If you have a command from God to do a certain thing, you need not inquire into the reason of the command, it is disobedient to begin to canvass God's will; but when there is no precept whatever, why persevere in an act which evidently does not promise to bring any blessing? Who bade them stand gazing up into heaven? If Christ had done so, then in Christ's name let them stand like statues and never turn their heads: but as he had not bidden them, why did they do what he had not commanded and leave undone what he had commanded? For he had strictly charged them that they should tarry at Jerusalem till they were "endued with power from on high." So what they did was not justifiable.

Here is the practical point for us: *what they did we are very apt to imitate.* "Oh," say you, "I shall never stand gazing up into heaven." I am not sure of that. Some Christians are very curious, but not obedient. Plain precepts are neglected, but difficult problems they seek to solve. I remember one who used always to be dwelling upon the vials and seals and trumpets. He was great at apocalyptic symbols; but he had seven children, and he had no family prayer. If he had left the vials and trumpets and minded his boys and girls, it would have been a deal better. I have known men marvelously great upon Daniel, and specially instructed in Ezekiel, but singularly forgetful of the twentieth of Exodus, and not very clear upon Romans the eighth. I do not speak with any blame of such folks for studying Daniel and Ezekiel, but quite the reverse; yet I wish they had been more zealous for the conversion of the sinners in their neighborhoods, and more careful to assist the poor saints. I admit the value of the study of the feet of the image in Nebuchadnezzar's vision, and the importance of knowing the kingdoms which make up the ten toes, but I do not see the propriety of allowing such studies to overlay the commonplaces of practical godliness. If the time spent over obscure theological propositions were given to a mission in the dim alley near the good man's house, more benefit would come to man and more glory to God. I would have you understand all mysteries, brethren, if you could; but do not forget that our chief business here below is to cry, "Behold the Lamb!" By all manner of means read and search till you know all that the Lord has revealed concerning things to come; but first of all see to it that your children are brought to the Savior's feet, and that you are workers together with God in the upbuilding of his church. The dense mass of misery and ignorance and sin which is round about us on every side demands all our powers; and if you do not respond to the call, though I am not a man in white apparel, I shall venture to say to you, "You men of Christendom, why stand you gazing up into the mysteries when so much is to be done for Jesus, and you are leaving it undone?" O you who are curious but not obedient, I fear I speak to you in vain, but I have spoken. May the Holy Spirit also speak.

Others are contemplative but not active, much given to the study of Scripture and to meditation thereon, but not zealous for good works. Contemplation is so scarce in these days that I could wish there were a thousand times as much of it; but in the case to which I refer everything runs in the one channel of thought, all time is spent in reading, in enjoyment, in rapture, in pious leisure. Religion never ought to become the subject of selfishness, and yet I fear some treat it as if its chief end was spiritual gratification. When a man's religion all lies in his saving his own self, and in enjoying holy things for his own self, there is a disease upon him. When his judgment of a sermon is based upon the one question, "Did it feed *me*?" it is a swinish judgment. There is such a thing as getting a swinish religion in which you are yourself first, yourself second, yourself third, yourself to the utmost end. Did Jesus ever think or speak in that fashion? Contemplation of Christ himself may be so carried out as to lead you away from Christ: the recluse meditates on Jesus, but he is as unlike the busy self-denying Jesus as well can be. Meditation unattended with active service in the spreading of the gospel among men, well deserves the rebuke of the angel, "Ye men of Galilee, why stand ye gazing up into heaven?"

Moreover, some are careful and anxious and deliriously impatient for some marvelous interposition. We get at times into a sad state of mind, because we do not see the kingdom of Christ advancing as we desire. I suppose it is with you as it is with me—I begin to fret, and I am deeply troubled, and I feel that there is good reason that I should be, for truth is fallen in the streets, and the days of blasphemy and rebuke are upon us. Then we pine; for the Master is away, and we cry, "When will he be back again? Oh, why are his chariots so long in coming? Why tarries he through the ages?" Our desires sour into impatience, and we commence gazing up into heaven, looking for his coming with a restlessness which does not allow us to discharge our duty as we should. Whenever anybody gets into that state, this is the word, "Ye men of Galilee, why stand ye gazing up into heaven?"

In certain cases this uneasiness has drawn to itself a wrong expectation of immediate wonders, and an intense desire for sign seeing. Ah me, what fanaticisms come of this! In America years ago, one came forward who declared that on such a day the Lord would come, and he led a great company to believe his crazy predictions. Many took their horses and fodder for two or three days and went out into the woods, expecting to be all the more likely to see all that was to be seen when once away from the crowded city. All over the States there were people who had made ascension dresses in which to soar into the air in proper costume. They waited, and they waited, and I am sure that no text could have been more appropriate for them than this, "You men of America, why stand you here gazing up into heaven?" Nothing came of it; and yet there are thousands in England and America who only need a fanatical leader, and they would run into the like folly. The desire to know the times and seasons is a craze with many poor bodies whose insanity runs in that particular groove. Every occurrence is a "sign of the times": a sign, I may add, which they do not understand. An earthquake is a special favorite with them. "Now," they cry, "the Lord is coming"; as if there had not been earthquakes of the sort we have heard of lately hundreds of times since our Lord went up into heaven. When the prophetic earthquakes occur in diverse places, we shall know of it without the warnings of these brethren. What a number of persons have been infatuated by the number of the beast and have been ready to leap for joy because they have found the number 666 in some great one's name. Why, everybody's name will yield that number if you treat it judiciously, and use the numerals of Greece, Rome, Egypt, China, or Timbuktu. I feel weary with the silly way in which some people make toys out of Scripture and play with texts as with a pack of cards. Whenever you meet with a man who sets up to be a prophet, keep out of his way in the future; and when you hear of signs and wonders, turn you to your Lord, and in patience possess your souls. "The just shall live by his faith." There is no other way of living among wild enthusiasts. Believe in God, and ask not for miracles and marvels, or the knowledge of times and seasons. To know when the Lord will restore the kingdom is not in your power. Remember that verse which I read just now in your hearing, "It is not for you to know the times or the seasons." If I were introduced into a room where a large number of parcels were stored up, and I was told that there was something good for me, I should begin to look for that which had my name upon it, and when I came upon a parcel and I saw in pretty big letters, "*It is not for you,*" I should leave it alone. Here, then, is a casket of knowledge marked, "*It is not for you* to know the times or the seasons, which the Father hath put in his own power." Cease to meddle with matters which are concealed and be satisfied to know the things which are clearly revealed.

**2. Second, I want you to notice** *the cheering description* **which these bright spirits give concerning our Lord. They describe him thus, "this same Jesus."**

I appreciate the description the more because *it came from those who knew him*. "He was seen of angels"; they had watched him all his life long, and they knew him, and when they, having just seen him rise to his Father and his God, said of him, "This same Jesus," then I know by an infallible testimony that he was the same, and that he is the same.

*Jesus is gone, but he still exists.* He has left us, but he is not dead; he has not dissolved into nothing like the mist of the morning. "This same Jesus" is gone up unto his Father's throne, and he is there today as certainly as he once stood at Pilate's bar. As surely as he did hang upon the cross, so surely does he, the selfsame man, sit upon the throne of God and reign over creation. I like to think of the positive identity of the Christ in the seventh heaven with the Christ in the lowest depths of agony. The Christ they spat upon is now the Christ whose name the cherubim and seraphim are hymning day without night. The Christ they scourged is he before whom principalities and powers delight to cast their crowns. Think of it and be glad this morning; and do not stand gazing up into heaven after a myth or a dream. Jesus lives; mind that you live also. Do not loiter as if you had nothing at all to do, or as if the kingdom of God had come to an end because Jesus is gone from the earth, as to his bodily presence. It is not all over; he still lives, and he has given you a work to do till he comes. Therefore, go and do it.

"This same Jesus"—I love that word, for "Jesus" means *a Savior*. O you anxious sinners here present, the name of him who has gone up into his glory is full of irritation to you! Will you not come to "this same Jesus"? This is he who opened the eyes of the blind and brought forth the prisoners out of the prison house. He is doing the same thing today. Oh, that your eyes may see his light! He that touched the lepers, and that raised the dead, is the same Jesus still, able to save to the uttermost. Oh, that you may look and live! You have only to come to him by faith, as she did who touched the hem of his garment; you have but to cry to him as the blind man did whose sight he restored; for he is the same Jesus, bearing about with him the same tender love for guilty men, and the same readiness to receive and cleanse all that come to him by faith.

"This same Jesus." Why, that must have meant that he who is in heaven is the same Christ who was on earth, but it must also mean that *he who is to come will be the same Jesus that went up into heaven.* There is no change in our blessed Master's nature, nor will there ever be. There is a great change in his condition:

> *The Lord shall come, but not the same*
> *As once in lowliness he came,*
> *A humble man before his foes,*
> *A weary man, and full of woes.*

He will be "the same Jesus" in nature though not in condition: he will possess the same tenderness when he comes to judge, the same gentleness of heart when all the glories of heaven and earth shall gird his brow. Our eye shall see him in that day, and we shall recognize him not only by the nail prints, but by the very look of his countenance, by the character that gleams from that marvelous face; and we shall say, "'Tis he! 'Tis he! the selfsame Christ that went up from the top of Olivet from the midst of his disciples." Go to him with your troubles, as you would have done when he was here. Look forward to his second coming without dread. Look for him with that joyous expectancy with which you would welcome Jesus of Bethany, who loved Mary, and Martha, and Lazarus.

On the back of that sweet title came this question, "Why stand ye here gazing into heaven?" They might have said, "We stay here because we do not know where to go. Our Master is gone." But oh, it is the same Jesus, and he is coming again, so go down to Jerusalem and get to work directly. Do not worry yourselves; no grave accident has occurred; it is not a disaster that Christ has gone, but an advance in his work. Despisers tell us nowadays, "Your cause is done for! Christianity is spun out! Your divine Christ is gone; we have not seen a trace of his miracle-working hand, nor of that voice which no man could rival." Here is our answer: we are not standing gazing up into heaven; we are not paralyzed because Jesus is away. He lives, the great Redeemer lives; and though it is our delight to lift up our eyes because we expect his coming, it is equally our delight to turn our heavenly gazing into an earthward watching, and to go down into the city, and there to tell that Jesus is risen, that men are to be saved by faith in him, and that whosoever believes in him shall have everlasting life. We are not defeated, far from it: his ascension is not a retreat, but an advance. His tarrying is not for want of power, but because of the abundance of his longsuffering. The victory is not questionable. All things work for it; all the hosts of God are mustering for the final charge. This same Jesus is mounting his white horse to lead forth the armies of heaven, conquering and to conquer.

3. Our third point is this, *the great practical truth*.

This truth is not one that is to keep us gazing into heaven, but one that is to make each of us go to his house to render earnest service. What is it?

Why, first, that *Jesus in gone into heaven*. Jesus is gone! Jesus is gone! It sounds like a knell. Jesus is taken up from you into heaven!—that sounds like a marriage peal. He is gone, but he is gone up to the hills, from which he can survey the battle; up to the throne, from which he can send us succor. The reserve forces of the Omnipotent stood waiting till their Captain came, and now that he is come into the center of the universe, he can send legions of angels, or he can raise up hosts of men for the help of his cause. I see every reason for going down into the world and getting to work, for he is gone up into heaven and "all power is given unto him in heaven and in earth." Is not that a good argument—"Go ye *therefore* and teach all nations, baptizing them in the name of the Father, and of the Son, and of the Holy Ghost"?

*Jesus will come again*. That is another reason for girding our loins, because it is clear that he has not quitted the fight, nor deserted the field of battle. Our great Captain is still heading the conflict; he has ridden into another part of the field, but he will be back again, perhaps in the twinkling of an eye. You do not say that a commander has given up the campaign because it is expedient that he should withdraw from your part of the field. Our Lord is doing the best thing for his kingdom in going away. It was in the highest degree expedient that he should go, and that we should each one receive the Spirit. There is a blessed unity between Christ the King and the commonest soldier in the ranks. He has not taken his heart from us, nor his care from us, nor his interest from us: he is bound up heart and soul with his people, and their holy warfare, and this is the evidence of it, "Behold, I come quickly; and my reward is with me, to give every man according as his work shall be."

Then, moreover, we are told in the text—and this is a reason why we should get to our work—*that he is coming in like manner as he departed*. Certain of the commentators do not seem to understand English at all. "He which is taken up from you into heaven shall so come in like manner as you have seen him go into heaven"; this, they say, relates to his spiritual coming at Pentecost. Give anybody a grain of sense, and do they not see that a spiritual coming is not a coming in the same manner in which he went up into heaven? There is an analogy, but certainly not a likeness between the two things. Our Lord was taken up; they could see him rise: he will come again, and "every eye shall see him." He went up not in spirit, but in person: he will come down in person. "This same Jesus shall so come in like manner." He went up as a matter of fact: not in poetic figure and spiritual symbol, but as a matter of fact, "this same Jesus" literally went up. "This same Jesus" will literally come again. He will descend in clouds even as he went up in clouds; and "he shall stand at the latter day upon the earth" even as he stood aforetime. He went up to heaven unopposed; no high priests nor scribes nor Pharisees nor even one of the rabble opposed his ascension; it were ridiculous to suppose that they could; and when he comes a second time none will stand against him. His adversaries shall perish; as the fat of rams shall they melt away in his presence. When he comes he shall break rebellious nations with a rod of iron, for his force shall be irresistible in that day.

Brethren, do not let anybody spiritualize away all this from you. Jesus is coming as a matter of fact, therefore go down to your sphere of service as a matter of fact. Get to work and teach the ignorant, win the wayward, instruct the children, and everywhere tell out the sweet name of Jesus. As a matter of fact, give of your substance and don't talk about it. As a matter of fact, consecrate your daily life to the glory of God. As a matter of fact, live wholly for your Redeemer. Jesus is not coming in a sort of mythical, misty, hazy way; he is literally and actually coming, and he will literally and actually call upon you to give an account of your stewardship. Therefore, now, today, literally not symbolically, personally and not by deputy, go out through that portion of the world which you can reach, and preach the gospel to every creature according as you have opportunity.

For this is what the men in white apparel meant—*be ready to meet your coming Lord*. What is the way to be ready to meet Jesus? If it is the same Jesus that went away from us who is coming, then let us be doing what he was doing before he went away. If it is the same Jesus that is coming, we cannot possibly put ourselves into a posture of which he will better approve than by going about doing good. If you would meet him with joy, serve him with earnestness. If the Lord Jesus Christ were to come today, I should like him to find me at my studying, praying, or preaching. Would you not like him to find you in your Sunday school, in your class, or out there at the corner of the street preaching, or doing whatever you have the privilege of doing in his name? Would you meet your Lord in idleness? Do not think of it. I called one day on one of our members, and she was whitening the front steps. She got up all in confusion; she said, "Oh dear, sir, I did not know you were coming today, or I would have been ready." I replied, "Dear friend, you could not be in better trim than you are: you are doing your duty like a good housewife, and may God bless you." She had no money to spare for a servant, and she was doing her duty by keeping the home tidy: I thought she looked more beautiful with her pail beside her than if she had been dressed according to the latest fashion. I said to her, "When the Lord Jesus Christ comes suddenly, I hope he will find me doing as you were doing, namely, fulfilling the duty of the hour." I want you all to get to your pails without being ashamed of them. Serve the Lord in some way or other; serve him always; serve him intensely; serve him more and more. Go tomorrow and serve the Lord at the counter, or in the workshop, or in the field. Go and serve the Lord by helping the poor and the needy, the widow and the fatherless; serve him by teaching the children, especially by endeavoring to train your own children. Go and hold a temperance meeting, and show the drunkard that there is hope for him in Christ, or go to the midnight meeting and let the fallen woman know that Jesus can restore her. Do what Jesus has given you the power to do, and then, you men of Britain, you will not stand gazing up into heaven, but you will wait upon the Lord in prayer, and you will receive the Spirit of God, and you will publish to all around the doctrine of "believe and live." Then when he comes, he will say to you, "Well done, good and faithful servant, enter thou into the joy of thy Lord." So may his grace enable us to do. Amen.

# Coming Judgment of the Secrets of Men

~⁂~

Delivered on Lord's Day morning, June 12, 1885, at the Metropolitan Tabernacle, Newington. No. 1849.

> *The day when God shall judge the secrets of men by Jesus Christ according to my gospel.* —Romans 2:16

It is impossible for any of us to tell what it cost the apostle Paul to write the first chapter of the Epistle to the Romans. It is a shame even to speak of the things which are done of the vicious in secret places; but Paul felt that it was necessary to break through his shame, and to speak out concerning the hideous vices of the heathen. He has left on record an exposure of the sins of his day which crimsons the cheek of the modest when they read it, and makes both the ears of him that hears it to tingle. Paul knew that this chapter would be read, not in his age alone, but in all ages, and that it would go into the households of the most pure and godly as long as the world should stand; and yet he deliberately wrote it, and wrote it under the guidance of the Holy Spirit. He knew that it must be written to put to shame the abominations of an age which was almost past shame. Monsters that revel in darkness must be dragged into the open, that they may be withered up by the light. After Paul has thus written in anguish he reminded himself of his chief comfort. While his pen was black with the words he had written in the first chapter, he was driven to write of his great delight. He clings to the gospel with a greater tenacity than ever. As in the verse before us he needed to mention the gospel, he did not speak of it as "the gospel," but as "*my gospel.*" "God shall judge the secrets of men by Jesus Christ, according to *my gospel.*" He felt that he could not live in the midst of so depraved a people without holding the gospel with both hands, and grasping it as his very own. "*My gospel,*" says he. Not that Paul was the author of it, not that Paul had an exclusive monopoly of its blessings, but that he had so received it from Christ himself, and regarded himself as so responsibly put in trust with it, that he could not disown it even for an instant. So fully had he taken it into himself that he could not do less than call it "my gospel." In another place he speaks of "our gospel"; thus using a possessive pronoun, to show how believers identify themselves with the truth which they preach. He had a gospel, a definite form of truth, and he believed in it beyond all doubt; and therefore he spoke of it as "my gospel." Herein we hear the voice of faith, which seems to say, "Though others reject it, I am sure of it, and allow no shade of mistrust to darken my mind. To me it is glad tidings of great joy: I hail it as 'my gospel.' If I be called a fool for holding it, I am content to be a fool, and to find all my wisdom in my Lord."

> *Should all the forms that men devise*
> *Assault my faith with treacherous art,*
> *I'd call them vanity and lies,*
> *And bind the gospel to my heart.*

Is not this word "my gospel" the voice of love? Does he not by this word embrace the gospel as the only love of his soul—for the sake of which he had suffered the loss of all things, and did count them but dung—for the sake of which he was willing to stand before Nero, and proclaim, even in Caesar's palace, the message from heaven? Though each word should cost him a life, he was willing to die a thousand deaths for the holy cause. "My gospel," says he, with a rapture of delight, as he presses to his bosom the sacred deposit of truth.

"My gospel." Does not this show his courage? As much as to say, "I am not ashamed of the gospel of Christ: for it is the power of God unto salvation to every one that believeth." He says, "my gospel," as a soldier speaks of "my colors" or of "my king." He resolves to bear this banner to victory, and to serve this royal truth even to the death.

"My gospel." There is a touch of discrimination about the expression. Paul perceives that there are other gospels, and he makes short work with them, for he says, "Though we, or an angel from heaven, preach any other gospel unto you than that which we have preached unto you, let him be accursed." The apostle was of a gentle spirit; he prayed heartily for the Jews who persecuted him, and yielded his life for the conversion of the Gentiles who maltreated him; but he had no tolerance for false preachers. He exhibited great breadth of mind, and to save souls he became all things to all men; but when he contemplated any alteration or adulteration of the gospel of Christ, he thundered and lightened without measure. When he feared that something else might spring up among the philosophers, or among the Judaizers, that should hide a single beam of the glorious Sun of righteousness, he used no measured language; but cried concerning the author of such a darkening influence, "Let him be accursed." Every heart that would see men blessed whispers an "amen" to the apostolic malediction. No greater curse can come upon mankind than the obscuration of the gospel of Jesus Christ. Paul says of himself and his true brethren, "We are not as many, which corrupt the word of God"; and he cries to those who turned aside from the one and only gospel, "O foolish Galatians, who hath bewitched you?" Of all new doctrines, he speaks as of "another gospel, which is not another; but there be some that trouble you."

As for myself, looking at the matter afresh, amid all the filthiness which I see in the world at this day, I lay hold upon the pure and blessed Word of God, and call it all the more earnestly, my gospel, mine in life and mine in death, mine against all comers, mine forever, God helping me: with emphasis—"my gospel."

Now let us notice what it was that brought up this expression, "my gospel." What was Paul preaching about? Certainly not upon any of the gentle and tender themes, which we are told nowadays ought to occupy all our time; but he is speaking of the terrors of the law, and in that connection he speaks of "my gospel."

Let us come at once to our text. It will need no dividing, for it divides itself. First, let us consider that *on a certain day God shall judge mankind;* second, on that day *God will judge the secrets of men;* third, when he judges the secrets of men, *it will be by Jesus Christ;* and fourth, *this is according to the gospel.*

## 1. We begin with the solemn truth, that *on a certain day God will judge men.*

A judgment is going on daily. God is continually holding court, and considering the doings of the sons of men. Every evil deed that they do is recorded in the register of doom, and each good action is remembered and laid up in store by God. That judgment is reflected in a measure in the consciences of men. Those who know the gospel, and those who know it not, alike, have a certain measure of light, by which they know right from wrong; their consciences all the while accusing or else excusing them. This session of the heavenly court continues from day to day, like that of our local magistrates; but this does not prevent but rather necessitates the holding of an ultimate great assize.

As each man passes into another world, there is an immediate judgment passed upon him; but this is only the foreshadowing of that which will take place in the end of the world.

There is a judgment also passing upon nations, for as nations will not exist as nations in another world, they have to be judged and punished in this present state. The thoughtful reader of history will not fail to observe, how sternly this justice has dealt with empire after empire, when they have become corrupt. Colossal dominions have withered to the ground, when sentenced by the King of kings. Go you and ask today, "Where is the empire of Assyria? Where are the mighty cities of Babylon? Where are the glories of the Medes and Persians? What has become of the Macedonian power? Where are the Caesars and their palaces?" These empires were forces established by cruelty and used for oppression; they fostered luxury and licentiousness, and when they were no longer tolerable, the earth was purged from their polluting existence. Ah me! what horrors of war, bloodshed, and devastation, have come upon men as the result of their iniquities! The world is full of the monuments, both of the mercy and the justice of God: in fact, the monuments of his justice, if rightly viewed, are proofs of his goodness; for it is mercy on the part of God to put an end to evil systems when, like a nightmare, they weigh heavily upon the bosom of mankind. The omnipotent Judge has not ceased from his sovereign rule over kingdoms, and our own country may yet have to feel his chastisements. We have often laughed among ourselves at the ridiculous idea of the New Zealander sitting on the broken arch of London Bridge amid the ruins of this metropolis. But is it quite so ridiculous as it looks? It is more than possible it will be realized if our iniquities continue to abound. What is there about London that it should be more enduring than Rome? Why should the palaces of *our* monarchs be eternal if the palaces of Koyunjik [in Assyria] have fallen? The almost boundless power of the pharaohs has passed away, and Egypt has become the meanest of nations; why should not England come under like condemnation? What are we? What is there about our boastful race, whether on this side of the Atlantic or the other, that we should monopolize the favor of God? If we rebel, and sin against him, he will not hold us guiltless, but will deal out impartial justice to an ungrateful race.

Still, though such judgments proceed every day, yet there is to be a day, a period of time, in which, in a more distinct, formal, public, and final manner, God will judge the sons of men. We might have guessed this by the light of nature and of reason. Even heathen peoples have had a dim notion of a day of doom; but we are not left to guess it, we are solemnly assured of it in Holy Scripture. Accepting this Book as the revelation of God, we know beyond all doubt that a day is appointed in which the Lord will judge the secrets of men.

By judging is here meant all that concerns the proceedings of trial and award. God will judge the race of men; that is to say, first, there will be a session of majesty, and the appearing of a great white throne, surrounded with pomp of angels and glorified beings. Then a summons will be issued, bidding all men come to judgment, to give in their final account. The heralds will fly through the realms of death, and summon those who sleep in the dust: for the quick and the dead shall all appear before that judgment seat. John says, "I saw the dead, small and great, stand before God"; and he adds, "The sea gave up the dead which were in it; and death and hell delivered up the dead which were in them." Those that have been so long buried that their dust is mingled with the soil, and has undergone a thousand transmutations, shall nevertheless be made to put in a personal appearance before the judgment seat of Christ. What an assize will that be! You and I and all the myriad myriads of our race shall be gathered before the throne of the Son of God. Then, when all are gathered, the indictment will be read, and each one will be examined concerning things done in the body, according to that he has done. Then the books shall be opened, and everything recorded there shall be read before the face of heaven. Every sinner shall then hear the story of his life published to his everlasting shame. The good shall ask no concealment, and the evil shall find none. Angels and men shall then see the truth of things, and the saints shall judge the world. Then the great Judge himself shall give the decision: he shall pronounce sentence upon the wicked, and execute their punishment. No partiality shall there be seen; there shall be no private conferences to secure immunity for nobles, no hushing up of matters, that great men may escape contempt for their crimes. All men shall stand before the one great judgment bar; evidence shall be given concerning them all, and a righteous sentence shall go forth from his mouth who knows not how to flatter the great.

This will be so, and it ought to be so: God should judge the world, because he is the universal ruler and sovereign. There has been a day for sinning, there ought to be a day for punishing; a long age of rebellion has been endured, and there must be a time when justice shall assert her supremacy. We have seen an age in which reformation has been commanded, in which mercy has been presented, in which expostulation and entreaty have been used, and there ought at last to come a day in which God shall judge both the quick and the dead, and measure out to each the final result of life. It ought to be so for the sake of the righteous. They have been slandered; they have been despised and ridiculed; worse than that, they have been imprisoned and beaten, and put to death times without number: the best have had the worst of it, and there ought to be a judgment to set these things right. Besides, the festering iniquities of each age cry out to God that he should deal with them. Shall such sin go unpunished? To what end is there a moral government at all, and how is its continuance to be secured, if there be not rewards and punishments and a day of account? For the display of his holiness, for the overwhelming of his adversaries, for the rewarding of those who have faithfully served him, there must be and shall be a day in which God will judge the world.

Why does it not come at once? And when will it come? The precise date we cannot tell. Man nor angel knows that day, and it is idle and profane to guess at it, since even the Son of man, as such, knows not the time. It is sufficient for us that the judgment day will surely come; sufficient also to believe that it is postponed on purpose to give breathing time for mercy, and space for repentance. Why should the ungodly want to know when that day will come? What is that day to you? To you it shall be darkness and not light. It shall be the day of your consuming as stubble fully dry: therefore bless the Lord that he delays his coming and reckon that his longsuffering is for your salvation.

Moreover, the Lord keeps the scaffold standing till he has built up the fabric of his church. Not yet are the elect all called out from among the guilty sons of men; not yet are all the redeemed with blood redeemed with power and brought forth out of the corruption of the age into the holiness in which they walk with God. Therefore the Lord waits for a while. But do not deceive yourselves. The great day of his wrath comes on apace, and your days of reprieve are numbered. One day is with the Lord as a thousand years, and a thousand years as one day. You shall die, perhaps, before the appearing of the Son of man; but you shall see his judgment seat for all that, for you shall rise again as surely as he rose. When the apostle addressed the Grecian sages at Athens he said, "God now commandeth all men everywhere to repent, because he has appointed a day, in the which he will judge the world in righteousness by that man whom he has ordained; whereof he has given assurance unto all men, in that he has raised him from the dead." See you not, O you impenitent ones, that a risen Savior is the sign of your doom. As God has raised Jesus from the dead, so shall he raise your bodies, that in these you may come to judgment. Before the judgment seat shall every man and woman in this house give an account of the things done in the body, whether they be good or whether they be evil. Thus says the Lord.

## 2. Now I call your attention to the fact that *"God will judge the secrets of men."*

This will happen to all men, of every nation, of every age, of every rank, and of every character. The Judge will, of course, judge their outward acts, but these may be said to have gone before them to judgment: their secret acts are specially mentioned, because these will make judgment to be the more searching.

By "the secrets of men," the Scripture means those secret crimes which hide themselves away by their own infamy, which are too vile to be spoken of, which cause a shudder to go through a nation if they be but dragged, as they ought to be, into the daylight. Secret offenses shall be brought into judgment; the deeds of the night and of the closed room, the acts which require the finger to be laid upon the lip, and a conspiracy of silence to be sworn. Revolting and shameless sins which must never be mentioned lest the man who committed them should be excluded from his fellows as an outcast, abhorred even of other sinners—all these shall be revealed. All that you have done, any one of you, or are doing, if you are bearing the Christian name and yet practicing secret sin, shall be laid bare before the universal gaze. If you sit here among the people of God, and yet where no eye sees you, if you are living in dishonesty, untruthfulness, or uncleanness, it shall all be known, and shame and confusion of face shall eternally cover you. Contempt shall be the inheritance to which you shall awake, when hypocrisy shall be no more possible. Be not deceived, God is not mocked; but he will bring the secrets of men into judgment.

Specially our text refers to the hidden motives of every action; for a man may do that which is right from a wrong motive, and so the deed may be evil in the sight of God, though it seem right in the sight of men. Oh, think what it will be to have your motives all brought to light, to have it proven that you were godly for the sake of gain, that you were generous out of ostentation, or zealous for love of praise, that you were careful in public to maintain a religious reputation, but that all the while everything was done for self, and self only! What a strong light will that be which God shall turn upon our lives, when the darkest chambers of human desire and motive shall be as manifest as public acts! What a revelation will that be which makes manifest all thoughts and imaginings and lustings and desires! All angers and envies and prides and rebellions of the heart—what a disclosure will these make!

All the sensual desires and imaginings of even the best regulated, what a foulness will these appear! What a day will it be, when the secrets of men shall be set in the full blaze of noon!

God will also reveal secrets that were secrets even to the sinners themselves, for there is sin in us which we have never seen and iniquity in us which we have never yet discovered.

We have managed for our own comfort's sake to blind our eyes somewhat, and we take care to avert our gaze from things which it is inconvenient to see; but we shall be compelled to see all these evils in that day, when the Lord shall judge the secrets of men. I do not wonder that when a certain rabbi read in the book of Ecclesiastes that God shall bring every work into judgment, with every secret thing, whether it be good, or whether it be evil, he wept. It is enough to make this best man tremble. Were it not for you, O Jesus, whose precious blood has cleansed us from all sin, where should we be! Were it not for your righteousness, which shall cover those who believe in you, who among us could endure the thought of that tremendous day? In you, O Jesus, we are made righteous, and therefore we fear not the trial hour, but were it not for you our hearts would fail us for fear!

Now if you ask me why God should judge, especially the secrets of men—since this is not done in human courts, and cannot be, for secret things of this kind come not under cognizance of our shortsighted tribunals—I answer it is because there is really nothing secret from God. We make a difference between secret and public sins, but he does not; for all things are naked and open to the eyes of him with whom we have to do. All deeds are done in the immediate presence of God, who is personally present everywhere. He knows and sees all things as one upon the spot, and every secret sin is but conceived to be secret through the deluded fantasy of our ignorance. God sees more of a secret sin than a man can see of that which is done before his face. "'Can any hide himself in secret places that I shall not see him?' saith the Lord."

The secrets of men will be judged because often the greatest of moral acts are done in secret. The brightest deeds that God delights in are those that are done by his servants when they have shut the door and are alone with him—when they have no motive but to please him; when they studiously avoid publicity, lest they should be turned aside by the praise of men; when the right hand knows not what the left hand does, and the loving, generous heart devises liberal things, and does it behind the screen, so that it should never be discovered how the deed was done. It were a pity that such deeds should be left out at the great audit. Thus, too, secret vices are also of the very blackest kind, and to exempt them were to let the worst of sinners go unpunished. Shall it be that these polluted beings shall escape because they have purchased silence with their wealth? I say solemnly, "God forbid." He does forbid it: what they have done in secret, shall be proclaimed upon the housetops.

Besides, the secret things of men enter into the very essence of their actions. An action is, after all, good or bad very much according to its motive. It may seem good, but the motive may taint it; and so, if God did not judge the secret part of the action, he would not judge righteously. He will weigh our actions, and detect the design which led to them, and the spirit which prompted them.

Is it not certainly true that the secret thing is the best evidence of the man's condition? Many a man will not do in public that which would bring him shame; not because he is not black-hearted enough for it, but because he is too much of a coward. That which a man does when he thinks that he is entirely by himself is the best revelation of the man. That which you will not do because it would be told of you if you did ill, is a poor index of your real character. That which you will do because you will be praised for doing well is an equally faint test of your heart. Such virtue is mere self-seeking or mean-spirited subservience to your fellowman; but that which you do out of respect to no authority but your own conscience and your God; that which you do unobserved, without regard to what man will say concerning it—that it is which reveals you, and discovers your real soul. Hence God lays a special stress and emphasis here upon the fact that he will in that day judge "the secrets" of men by Jesus Christ.

O friends, if it does not make you tremble to think of these things, it ought to do so. I feel the deep responsibility of preaching upon such matters, and I pray God of his infinite mercy to apply these truths to our hearts, that they may be forceful upon our lives. These truths ought to startle us, but I am afraid we hear them with small result; we have grown familiar with them, and they do not penetrate us as they should. We have to deal, brethren, with an omniscient God; with One who once knowing never forgets; with One to whom all things are always present; with One who will conceal nothing out of fear or favor of any man's person; with One who will shortly bring the splendor of his omniscience and the impartiality of his justice to bear upon all human lives. God help us, wherever we rove and wherever we rest, to remember that each thought, word, and act of each moment lies in that fierce light which beats upon all things from the throng of God.

### 3. Another solemn revelation of our text lies in this fact, that *"God will judge the secrets of men by Jesus Christ."*

He that will sit upon the throne as the vicegerent of God, and as a judge, acting for God, will be Jesus Christ. What a name for a judge! The Savior-Anointed—Jesus Christ: he is to be the Judge of all mankind. Our Redeemer will be the umpire of our destiny.

This will be, I doubt not, first for the display of his glory. What a difference there will be then between the babe of Bethlehem's manger, hunted by Herod, carried down by night into Egypt for shelter, and the King of kings and Lord of lords, before whom every knee must bow! What a difference between the weary man and full of woes, and he that shall then be girded with glory, sitting on a throne encircled with a rainbow! From the derision of men to the throne of universal judgment, what an ascent! I am unable to convey to you my own heart's sense of the contrast between the "despised and rejected of men," and the universally acknowledged Lord, before whom Caesar and pontiffs shall bow into the dust. He who was judged at Pilate's bar shall summon all to his bar. What a change from the shame and spitting, from the nails and the wounds, the mockery and the thirst, and the dying anguish, to the glory in which he shall come whose eyes are as a flame of fire, and out of whose mouth there goes a two-edged sword! He shall judge the nations, even he whom the nations abhorred. He shall break them in pieces like a potter's vessel, even those who cast him out as unworthy to live among them. Oh, how we ought to bow before him now as he reveals himself in his tender sympathy and in his generous humiliation! Let us kiss the Son lest he be angry; let us yield to his grace, that we may not be crushed by his wrath. You sinners, bow before those pierced feet, which else will tread you like clusters in the winepress. Look you up to him with weeping, and confess your forgetfulness of him, and put your trust in him; lest he look down on you in indignation. Oh, remember that he will one day say, "But those mine enemies, which would not that I should reign over them, bring hither, and slay them before me." The holding of the judgment by the Lord Jesus will greatly enhance his glory. It will finally settle one controversy which is still upheld by certain erroneous spirits: there will be no doubt about our Lord's deity in that day: there will be no question that this same Jesus who was crucified is both Lord and God. God himself shall judge, but he shall perform the judgment in the person of his Son Jesus Christ, truly man, but nevertheless most truly God. Being God he is divinely qualified to judge the world in righteousness, and the people with his truth.

If you ask again, "Why is the Son of God chosen to be the final Judge?" I could give as a further answer that he receives this high office not only as a reward for all his pains, and as a manifestation of his glory, but also because men have been under his mediatorial sway, and he is their Governor and King. At the present moment we are all under the sway of the Prince Emmanuel, God with us: we have been placed by an act of divine clemency, not under the immediate government of an offended God, but under the reconciling rule of the Prince of peace. "All power is given unto him in heaven and in earth." "The Father judgeth no man, but hath committed all judgment unto the Son: that all men should honor the Son, even as they honor the Father." We are commanded to preach unto the people, and "to testify that it is he which was ordained of God to be the Judge of quick and dead" (Acts 10:42). Jesus is our Lord and King, and it is meet that he should conclude his mediatorial sovereignty by rewarding his subjects according to their deeds.

But I have somewhat to say unto you which ought to reach your hearts, even if other thoughts have not done so. I think that God has chosen Christ, the man Christ Jesus, to judge the world that there may never be a cavil raised concerning that judgment. Men shall not be able to say—we were judged by a superior being who did not know our weaknesses and temptations, and therefore he judged us harshly, and without a generous consideration of our condition. No, God shall judge the secrets of men by Jesus Christ, who was tempted in all points like as we are, yet without sin. He is our brother, bone of our bone and flesh of our flesh, partaker of our humanity, and therefore understands and knows what is in men. He has shown himself to be skillful in all the surgery of mercy throughout the ages, and at last he will be found equally skillful in dissecting motives and revealing the thoughts and intents of the heart. Nobody shall ever be able to look back on that august tribunal and say that he who sat upon it was too stern, because he knew nothing of human weakness. It will be the loving Christ, whose tears and bloody sweat and gaping wounds attest his brotherhood with mankind; and it will be clear to all intelligences that however dread his sentences, he could not be unmerciful. God shall judge us by Jesus Christ, that the judgment may be indisputable.

But hearken well—for I speak with a great weight upon my soul—this judgment by Christ Jesus puts beyond possibility all hope of any after-interposition. If the Savior condemns, and such a Savior, who can plead for us? The owner of the vineyard was about to cut down the barren tree, when the dresser of the vineyard pleaded, "Let it alone this year also"; but what can come of that tree when the vinedresser himself shall say to the master, "It must fall; I myself must cut it down"! If your Savior shall become your Judge, you will be judged indeed. If he shall say, "Depart, you cursed," who can call you back? If he that bled to save men at last comes to this conclusion, that there is no more to be done, but they must be driven from his presence, then farewell hope. To the guilty the judgment will indeed be a "great day of dread, decision, and despair."

An infinite horror shall seize upon their spirits as the words of the loving Christ shall freeze their very marrow, and fix them in the ice of eternal despair. There is, to my mind, a climax of solemnity in the fact that God shall judge the secrets of men by Jesus Christ.

Does not this also show how certain the sentence will be? for this Christ of God is too much in earnest to play with men. If he says, "Come, you blessed," he will not fail to bring them to their inheritance. If he be driven to say, "Depart, you cursed," he will see it done, and into the everlasting punishment they must go. Even when it cost him his life, he did not draw back from doing the will of his Father, nor will he shrink in that day when he shall pronounce the sentence of doom. Oh, how evil must sin be since it constrains the tender Savior to pronounce sentence of eternal woe! I am sure that many of us have been driven of late to an increased hatred of sin; our souls have recoiled within us because of the wickedness among which we dwell; it has made us feel as if we would fain borrow the Almighty's thunderbolts with which to smite iniquity. Such haste on our part may not be seemly, since it implies a complaint against divine longsuffering; but Christ's dealing with evil will be calm and dispassionate, and all the more crushing. Jesus, with his pierced hand, that bears the attestation of his supreme love to men, shall wave the impenitent away; and those lips which bade the weary rest in him shall solemnly say to the wicked, "Depart, you cursed, into everlasting fire prepared for the devil and his angels." To be trampled beneath the foot which was nailed to the cross will be to be crushed indeed: yet so it is, God shall judge the secrets of men by Jesus Christ.

It seems to me as if God in this intended to give a display of the unity of all his perfections. In this same man, Christ Jesus, the Son of God, you behold justice and love, mercy and righteousness, combined in equal measure. He turns to the right, and says, "Come, you blessed," with infinite suavity; and with the same lip, as he glances to the left, he says, "Depart, you cursed." Men will then see at one glance how love and righteousness are one, and how they meet in equal splendor in the person of the well beloved, whom God has therefore chosen to be Judge of quick and dead.

**4. I have done when you have borne with me a minute or two upon my next point, which is this: and** *all this is according to the gospel.*

That is to say, there is nothing in the gospel contrary to this solemn teaching. Men gather to us, to hear us preach of infinite mercy, and tell of the love that blots out sin; and our task is joyful when we are called to deliver such a message; but O sirs, remember that nothing in our message makes light of sin. The gospel offers you no opportunity of going on in sin, and escaping without punishment. Its own cry is, "Except ye repent, ye shall all likewise perish." Jesus has not come into the world to make sin less terrible. Nothing in the gospel excuses sin; nothing in it affords toleration for lust or anger or dishonesty or falsehood. The gospel is as truly a two-edged sword against sin, as ever the law can be. There is grace for the man who quits his sin, but there is tribulation and wrath upon every man that does evil. "If ye turn not he will whet his sword; he hath bent his bow, and made it ready." The gospel is all tenderness to the repenting, but all terror to the obstinate offender. It has pardon for the very chief of sinners, and mercy for the vilest of the vile, if they will forsake their sins; but it is according to our gospel that he that goes on in his iniquity, shall be cast into hell, and he that believes not shall be damned. With deep love to the souls of men, I bear witness to the truth that he who turns not with repentance and faith to Christ shall go away into punishment as everlasting as the life of the righteous. This is according to our gospel: indeed, we had not needed such a gospel, if there had not been such a judgment. The background of the cross is the judgment seat of Christ. We had not needed so great an atonement, so vast a sacrifice, if there had not been an exceeding sinfulness in sin, an exceeding justice in the judgment, and an exceeding terror in the sure rewards of transgression.

"According to my gospel," says Paul; and he meant that the judgment is an essential part of the gospel creed. If I had to sum up the gospel, I should have to tell you certain facts: Jesus, the Son of God, became man; he was born of the Virgin Mary; lived a perfect life; was falsely accused of men, was crucified, dead, and buried; the third day he rose again from the dead; he ascended into heaven and sits on the right hand of God; from whence he shall also come to judge the quick and the dead. This is one of the elementary truths of our gospel; we believe in the resurrection of the dead, the final judgment, and the life everlasting.

The judgment is according to our gospel, and in times of righteous indignation its terrible significance seems a very gospel to the pure in heart. I mean this. I have read this and that concerning oppression, slavery, the treading down of the poor, and the shedding of blood, and I have rejoiced that there is a righteous judge. I have read of secret wickedness among the rich men of this city, and I have said within myself, "Thank God, there will be a judgment day." Thousands of men have been hanged for much less crimes than those which now disgrace gentlemen whose names are on the lips of rank and beauty. Ah me, how heavy is our heart as we think of it! It has come like a gospel to us that the Lord will be revealed in flaming fire, taking vengeance on them that know not God, and that obey not the gospel of our Lord Jesus Christ (2 Thess. 1:8). The secret wickedness of London cannot go on forever. Even they that love men best, and most desire salvation for them, cannot but cry to God, "How long! How long! Great God, will you forever endure this?" God has appointed a day in which he will judge the world, and we sigh and cry until it shall end the reign of wickedness, and give rest to the oppressed. Brethren, we must preach the coming of the Lord, and preach it somewhat more than we have done; because it is the driving power of the gospel. Too many have kept back these truths, and thus the bone has been taken out of the arm of the gospel. Its point has been broken; its edge has been blunted. The doctrine of judgment to come is the power by which men are to be aroused. There is another life; the Lord will come a second time; judgment will arrive; the wrath of God will be revealed. Where this is not preached, I am bold to say the gospel is not preached. It is absolutely necessary to the preaching of the gospel of Christ that men be warned as to what will happen if they continue in their sins. Ho, ho, sir surgeon, you are too delicate to tell the man that he is ill! You hope to heal the sick without their knowing it. You therefore flatter them; and what happens? They laugh at you; they dance upon their own graves. At last they die! Your delicacy is cruelty; your flatteries are poisons; you are a murderer. Shall we keep men in a fool's paradise? Shall we lull them into soft slumbers from which they will awake in hell? Are we to become helpers of their damnation by our smooth speeches? In the name of God, we will not. It becomes every true minister of Christ to cry aloud and spare not, for God has set a day in which he will "judge the secrets of men by Jesus Christ according to my gospel." As surely as Paul's gospel was true, the judgment will come. Wherefore flee to Jesus this day, O sinners. O you saints, come hide yourselves again beneath the crimson canopy of the atoning sacrifice, that you may be now ready to welcome your descending Lord and escort him to his judgment seat. O my hearers, may God bless you, for Jesus' sake. Amen.

# The Two Appearings and the Discipline of Grace

―❦―

Delivered on Lord's Day morning, April 4, 1886, at the Metropolitan Tabernacle, Newington. No. 1894.

> *For the grace of God that bringeth salvation hath appeared to all men, teaching us that, denying ungodliness and worldly lusts, we should live soberly, righteously, and godly, in this present world; looking for that blessed hope, and the glorious appearing of the great God and our Savior Jesus Christ; who gave himself for us, that he might redeem us from all iniquity, and purify unto himself a peculiar people, zealous of good works.* —TITUS 2:11–14

Upon reading this text one sees at a glance that Paul believed in a divine Savior. He did not preach a Savior who was a mere man. He believed the Lord Jesus Christ to be truly man, but he also believed him to be God over all, and he therefore uses the striking words, "the glorious appearing of the great God and our Savior Jesus Christ." There is no appearing of God the Father; there is no such expression in Scripture; the appearing is the appearing of that second person of the blessed Trinity in unity who has already once appeared, and who will appear a second time without a sin offering unto salvation in the latter days. Paul believed in Jesus as "the great God and our Savior." It was his high delight to extol the Lord who once was crucified in weakness. He calls him here, "the great God," thus specially dwelling upon his power, dominion, and glory; and this is the more remarkable because he immediately goes on to say, "who gave himself for us, that he might redeem us from all iniquity." He that gave himself, he that surrendered life itself upon the accursed tree, he that was stripped of all honor and glory and entered into the utmost depths of humiliation, was assuredly the great God notwithstanding all. O brothers, if you take away the deity of Christ what in the gospel is left that is worth the preaching? None but the great God is equal to the work of being our Savior.

We learn also at first sight that Paul believed in a great redemption. "Who gave himself for us that he might redeem us from all iniquity." That word "redemption" sounds in my ears like a silver bell. We are ransomed, purchased back from slavery, and this at an immeasurable price; not merely by the obedience of Christ, nor the suffering of Christ, nor even the death of Christ, but by Christ's giving himself for us. All that there is in the great God and Savior was paid down that he might "redeem us from all iniquity." The splendor of the gospel lies in the redeeming sacrifice of the Son of God, and we shall never fail to put this to the front in our preaching. It is the gem of all the gospel gems. As the moon is among the stars, so is this great doctrine among all the lesser lights which God has kindled to make glad the night of fallen man. Paul never hesitates; he has a divine Savior and a divine redemption, and he preaches these with unwavering confidence. Oh, that all preachers were like him!

It is also clear that Paul looked upon the appearing of the Savior as a Redeemer from all iniquity as a display of the grace of God. He says, "The grace of God that bringeth salvation hath appeared to all men." In the person of Christ the grace of God is revealed, as when the sun arises and makes glad all lands. It is not a private vision of God to a favored prophet on the lone mountain's brow; but it is an open declaration of the grace of God to every creature under heaven—a display of the grace of God to all eyes that are open to behold it. When the Lord Jesus Christ came to Bethlehem, and when he closed a perfect life by death upon Calvary, he manifested the grace of God more gloriously than has been done by creation or providence. This is the clearest revelation of the everlasting mercy of the living God. In the Redeemer we behold the unveiling of the Father's face. What if I say the laying bare of the divine heart? To repeat the figure of the text, this is the Dayspring from on high which has visited us: the Sun which has arisen with healing in his wings. The grace of God has shone forth conspicuously, and made itself visible to men of every rank in the person and work of the Lord Jesus. This was not given us because of any deserving on our part; it is a manifestation of free, rich, undeserved grace, and of that grace in its fullness. The grace of God has been made manifest to the entire universe in the appearing of Jesus Christ our Lord.

The grand object of the manifestation of divine grace in Christ Jesus is to deliver men from the dominion of evil. The world in Paul's day was sunk in immorality, debauchery, ungodliness, bloodshed, and cruelty of every kind. I have not time this morning to give you even an outline sketch of the Roman world when Paul wrote this letter to Titus. We are bad enough now; but the outward manners and customs of that period were simply horrible. The spread of the gospel has worked a change for the better. In the apostle's days the favorite spectacles for holiday entertainment were the butcheries of men; and such was the general depravity that vices which we hardly dare to mention were defended and gloried in. In the midnight of the world's history, our Lord appeared to put away sin. The Lord Jesus Christ, who is the manifestation of the divine grace to men, came into the world to put an end to the unutterable tyranny of evil. His work and teaching are meant to uplift mankind at large and also to redeem his people from all iniquity, and to sanctify them to himself as his peculiar heritage.

Paul looks upon recovery from sin as being a wonderful proof of divine grace. He does not talk about a kind of grace that would leave men in sin, and yet save them from its punishment. No, his salvation is salvation from sin. He does not talk about a free grace which winks at iniquity, and makes nothing of transgression; but of a greater grace by far, which denounces the iniquity and condemns the transgression, and then delivers the victim of it from the habit which has brought him into bondage. He declares that the grace of God has shone upon the world in the work of Jesus, in order that the darkness of its sin and ignorance may disappear, and the brightness of holiness and righteousness and peace, may rule the day. God send us to see these blessed results in every part of the world! God make us to see them in ourselves! May we ourselves feel that the grace of God has appeared to us individually! Our apostle would have Titus know that this grace was intended for all ranks of men, for the Cretans who were "always liars, evil beasts, slow bellies"; and even for the most despised bond slaves, who under the Roman Empire were treated worse than dogs. To each one of us, whether rich or poor, prominent or obscure, the gospel has come, and its design is that we may be delivered by it from all ungodliness and worldly lusts.

This being the run of the text, I ask you to come closer to it, while I try to show how the apostle stimulates us to holiness and urges us to overcome all evil. First, he describes *our position*; second, he describes *our instruction*; and, third, he mentions *our encouragements*. May the good Spirit bless our meditations at this hour!

## 1. First of all, the apostle in this text describes *our position*.

The people of God stand between two appearances. In the eleventh verse he tells us that "the grace of God that bringeth salvation hath appeared to all men"; and then he says, in the thirteenth verse, "Looking for that blessed hope, and the glorious appearing of the great God and our Savior Jesus Christ." We live in an age which is an interval between two appearings of the Lord from heaven. Believers in Jesus are shut off from the old economy by the first coming of our Lord. The times of man's ignorance God winked at, but now commands all men everywhere to repent. We are divided from the past by a wall of light, upon whose forefront we read the words "Bethlehem, Gethsemane, Calvary." We date from the birth of the Virgin's Son: we begin with *Anno Domini*. All the rest of time is before Christ, and is marked off from the Christian era. Bethlehem's manger is our beginning. The chief landmark in all time to us is the wondrous life of him who is the Light of the world. We look to the appearing of the grace of God in the form of the lowly One of Nazareth, for our trust is there. We confide in him who was made flesh and dwelt among us, so that men beheld his glory, the glory as of the only begotten of the Father, full of grace and truth. The dense darkness of the heathen ages begins to be broken when we reach the first appearing, and the dawn of a glorious day begins.

Brethren, we look forward to a second appearing. Our outlook for the close of this present era is another appearing—an appearing of glory rather than of grace. After our Master rose from the brow of Olivet, his disciples remained for a while in mute astonishment; but soon an angelic messenger reminded them of prophecy and promise by saying, "Ye men of Galilee, why stand ye gazing up into heaven? this same Jesus, which is taken up from you into heaven, shall so come in like manner as ye have seen him go into heaven." We believe that our Lord in the fullness of time will descend from heaven with a shout, with the trump of the archangel, and the voice of God.

> *The Lord shall come! the earth shall quake;*
> *The mountains to their center shake;*
> *And, withering from the vault of night,*
> *The stars shall pale their feeble light.*

This is the terminus of the present age. We look from *Anno Domini,* in which he came the first time, to that greater *Anno Domini,* or year of our Lord, in which he shall come a second time, in all the splendor of his power, to reign in righteousness, and break the evil powers as with a rod of iron.

See, then, where we are: we are compassed about, behind and before, with the appearings of our Lord. Behind us is our trust; before us is our hope. Behind us is the Son of God in humiliation; before us is the great God our Savior in his glory. To use an ecclesiastical term, we stand between two epiphanies: the first is the manifestation of the Son of God in human flesh in dishonor and weakness; the second is the manifestation of the same Son of God in all his power and glory. In what a position, then, do the saints stand! They have an era all to themselves which begins and ends with the Lord's appearing.

Our position is further described in the text, if you look at it, as being *in this present world,* or age. We are living in the age which lies between the two blazing beacons of the divine appearings; and we are called to hasten from one to the other. The sacramental host of God's elect is marching on from the one appearing to the other with hasty foot. We have everything to hope for in the last appearing, as we have everything to trust to in the first appearing; and we have now to wait with patient hope throughout that weary interval which intervenes. Paul calls it "this present world." This marks its fleeting nature. It is present, but it is scarcely future; for the Lord may come so soon, and thus end it all. It is present now, but it will not be present long. It is but a little time, and he that will come shall come and will not tarry. Now it is this "present world"; oh, how present it is! How sadly it surrounds us! Yet by faith we count these present things to be unsubstantial as a dream; and we look to the things which are not seen, and not present, as being real and eternal. We pass through this world as men on pilgrimage. We traverse an enemy's country. Going from one manifestation to another, we are as birds migrating on the wing from one region to another: there is no rest for us by the way. We are to keep ourselves as loose as we can from this country through which we make our pilgrim way; for we are strangers and foreigners, and here we have no continuing city. We hurry through this Vanity Fair: before us lies the Celestial City and the coming of the Lord who is the King thereof. As voyagers cross the Atlantic, and so pass from shore to shore, so do we speed over the waves of this ever-changing world to the glory land of the bright appearing of our Lord and Savior Jesus Christ.

Already I have given to you, in this description of our position, the very best argument for a holy life. If it be so, my brethren, you are not of the world even as Jesus is not of the world. If this be so, that before you blazes the supernatural splendor of the second advent, and behind you burns the everlasting light of the Redeemer's first appearing, what manner of people ought you to be? If, indeed, you be but journeying through this present world, suffer not your hearts to be defiled with its sins; learn not the manner of speech of these aliens through whose country you are passing. Is it not written, "The people shall dwell alone, and shall not be reckoned among the nations"? "Come ye out from among them, and be ye separate, touch not the unclean thing," for the Lord has said, "I will be a Father unto you, and ye shall be my sons and daughters." They that lived before the coming of Christ had responsibilities upon them, but not such as those which rest upon you who have seen the face of God in Jesus Christ, and who expect to see that face again. You live in light which renders their brightest knowledge a comparative darkness: walk as children of light. You stand between two mornings, between which there is no evening. The glory of the Lord has risen upon you once in the incarnation and atonement of your Lord: that light is shining more and more, and soon there will come the perfect day, which shall be ushered in by the second advent. The sun shall no more go down, but it shall unveil itself, and shed an indescribable splendor upon all hearts that look for it. "Put on therefore the armor of light." What a grand expression! Helmet of light, breastplate of light, shoes of light—everything of light. What a knight must he be who is clad, not in steel, but in light, light which shall flash confusion on his foes! There ought to be a holy light about you, O believer in Jesus, for there is the appearing of grace behind you, and the appearing of glory before you. Two manifestations of God shine upon you. Like a wall of fire the Lord's appearings are round about you: there ought to be a special glory of holiness in the midst. "Let your light so shine before men, that they may see your good works, and glorify your Father which is in heaven." That is the position of the righteous according to my text, and it furnishes a loud call to holiness.

**2. Second, I have to call your attention to *the instruction* which is given to us by the grace of God which has appeared unto all men.**

Our translation runs thus: "The grace of God hath appeared to all men, teaching us that, denying ungodliness and worldly lusts, we should live soberly, righteously, and godly, in this present world." A better translation would be: "The grace of God that brings salvation has appeared to all men, disciplining us in order that we may deny ungodliness and worldly lusts." Those of you who know a little Greek will note that the word which in our version is rendered "teaching" is a scholastic term, and has to do with the education of children; not merely the teaching, but the training and bringing of them up. The grace of God has come to be a schoolmaster to us, to teach us, to train us, to prepare us for a more developed state. Christ has manifested in his own person that wonderful grace of God which is to deal with us as with sons, and to educate us unto holiness, and so to the full possession of our heavenly heritage. We are the many sons who are to be brought to glory by the discipline of grace.

So then, first of all, *grace has a discipline.* We generally think of law when we talk about schoolmasters and discipline; but grace itself has a discipline and a wonderful training power too. The manifestation of grace is preparing us for the manifestation of glory. What the law could not do, grace is doing. The free favor of God instills new principles, suggests new thoughts, and by inspiring us with gratitude, creates in us love to God and hatred of that which is opposed to God. Happy are they who go to school to the grace of God! This grace of God entering into us shows us what was evil even more clearly than the commandment does. We receive a vital, testing principle within, whereby we discern between good and evil. The grace of God provides us with instruction, but also with chastisement, as it is written, "As many as I love I rebuke and chasten." As soon as we come under the conscious enjoyment of the free grace of God, we find it to be a holy rule, a fatherly government, a heavenly training. We find, not self-indulgence, much less licentiousness; but on the contrary, the grace of God both restrains and constrains us; it makes us free to holiness and delivers us from the law of sin and death by "the law of the spirit of life in Christ Jesus."

Grace has its discipline, *and grace has its chosen disciples,* for you cannot help noticing that while the eleventh verse says that, "the grace of God that brings salvation has appeared to all men," yet it is clear that this grace of God has not exercised its holy discipline upon all men, and therefore the text changes its "all men" into "us." Usually in Scripture when you get a generality you soon find a particularity near it. The text has it, "teaching us that, denying ungodliness and worldly lusts, we should live soberly, righteously, and godly, in this present world." Thus you see that grace has its own disciples. Are you a disciple of the grace of God? Did you ever come and submit yourself to it? Have you learned to spell that word "faith"? Have you childlike trust in Jesus? Have you learned to wash in the laver of atonement? Have you learned those holy exercises which are taught by the grace of God? Can you say that your salvation is of grace? Do you know the meaning of that text, "By grace are ye saved through faith; and that not of yourselves: it is the gift of God"? If so, then you are his disciples, and the grace of God which has appeared so conspicuously has come to discipline you. As the disciples of grace, endeavor to adorn its doctrine. According to the previous verses, even a slave might do this. He might be an ornament to the grace of God. Let grace have such an effect upon your life and character that all may say, "See what grace can do! See how the grace of God produces holiness in believers!" All along I wish to be driving at the point which the apostle is aiming at: that we are to be holy—holy because grace exercises a purifying discipline, and because we are the disciples of that grace.

*The discipline of grace, according to the apostle, has three results—denying, living, looking.* You see the three words before you. The first is "denying." When a young man comes to college he usually has much to unlearn. If his education has been neglected, a sort of instinctive ignorance covers his mind with briars and brambles. If he has gone to some faulty school where the teaching is flimsy, his tutor has first of all to fetch out of him what he has been badly taught. The most difficult part of the training of young men is not to put the right thing into them, but to get the wrong thing out of them. A man proposes to teach a language in six months, and in the end a great thing is done if one of his pupils is able to forget all his nonsense in six years. When the Holy Spirit comes into the heart, he finds that we know so much already of what it were well to leave unknown; we are self-conceited, we are puffed up. We have learned lessons of worldly wisdom and carnal policy, and these we need to unlearn and deny. The Holy Spirit works this denying in us by the discipline of grace.

What have we to deny? First, we have to deny ungodliness. That is a lesson which many of you have great need to learn. Listen to working men. "Oh," they say, "we have to work hard, we cannot think about God or religion." This is ungodliness! The grace of God teaches us to deny this; we come to loathe such atheism. Others are prospering in the world, and they cry, "If you had as much business to look after as I have, you would have no time to think about your soul or another world. Trying to battle with the competition of the times leaves me no opportunity for prayer or Bible reading; I have enough to do with my daybook and ledger." This also is ungodliness! The grace of God leads us to deny this; we abhor such forgetfulness of God. A great work of the Holy Spirit is to make a man godly, to make him think of God, to make him feel that this present life is not all, but that there is a judgment to come, wherein he must give an account before God. God cannot be forgotten with impunity. If we treat him as if he were nothing, and leave him out of our calculations for life, we shall make a fatal mistake. O my hearer, there is a God, and as surely as you live, you are accountable to him. When the Spirit of God comes with the grace of the gospel, he removes our inveterate ungodliness, and causes us to deny it with joyful earnestness.

We next deny "worldly lusts": that is, the lusts of the present world or age, which I described to you just now as coming in between the two appearings. This present age is as full of evil lusts as that in which Paul wrote concerning the Cretans. The lust of the eye, the lust of the flesh, and the pride of life are yet with us. Wherever the grace of God comes effectually, it makes the loose liver deny the desires of the flesh; it causes the man who lusted after gold to conquer his greediness; it brings the proud man away from his ambitions; it trains the idler to diligence, and it sobers the wanton mind which cared only for the frivolities of life. Not only do we leave these lusts, but we deny them. We have an abhorrence of those things wherein we formerly placed our delight. Our cry is, "What have I to do any more with idols?" To the worldling we say, "These things may belong to you; but as for us, we cannot own them; sin shall no more have dominion over us. We are not of the world, and therefore its ways and fashions are none of ours." The period in which we live shall have no paramount influence over us, for our truest life is with Christ in eternity; our conversation is in heaven. The grace of God has made us deny the prevailing philosophies, glories, maxims, and fashions of this present world. In the best sense we are nonconformists. We desire to be crucified to the world and the world to us. This was a great thing for grace to do among the degraded sensualists of Paul's day, and it is not a less glorious achievement in these times.

But then, brethren, you cannot be complete with a merely negative religion; you must have something positive; and so the next word is *living*—that "we should live soberly, righteously, and godly, in this present world." Observe, brethren, that the Holy Ghost expects us to live in this present world, and therefore we are not to exclude ourselves from it. This age is the battlefield in which the soldier of Christ is to fight. Society is the place in which Christianity is to exhibit the graces of Christ. If it were possible for these good sisters to retire into a large house and live secluded from the world, they would be shirking their duty rather than fulfilling it. If all the good men and true were to form a select colony, and do nothing else but pray and hear sermons, they would simply be refusing to serve God in his own appointed way. No, you have to live soberly, godly, righteously in this world, such as it is at present. It is of no use for you to scheme to escape from it. You are bound to breast this torrent, and buffet all its waves. If the grace of God is in you, that grace is meant to be displayed, not in a select and secluded retreat but in this present world. You are to shine in the darkness like a light.

This life is described in a threefold way. You are, first, to live "soberly"—that is, for yourself. "Soberly" in all your eating and your drinking, and in the indulgence of all bodily appetites—that goes without saying. Drunkards and gluttons, fornicators and adulterers, cannot inherit the kingdom of God. You are to live soberly in all your thinking, all your speaking, all your acting. There is to be sobriety in all your worldly pursuits. You are to have yourself well in hand: you are to be self-restrained. I know some brethren who are not often sober. I do not accuse them of being drunk with wine; but they are mentally intoxicated: they have no reason, no moderation, no judgment. They are all spur and no rein. Right or wrong, they must have that which they have set their hearts upon. They never look round to take the full bearing of a matter: they never estimate calmly; but with closed eyes they rush on like bulls. Alas for these unsober people! They are not to be depended on, they are everything by turns, and nothing long. The man who is disciplined by the grace of God becomes thoughtful, considerate, self-contained; and he is no longer tossed about by passion, or swayed by prejudice. There is only one insobriety into which I pray we may fall; and truth to say, that is the truest sobriety. Of this the Scripture says, "Be not drunk with wine, wherein is excess; but be filled with the Spirit." When the Spirit of God takes full possession of us, then we are borne along by his sacred energy, and are filled with a divine enthusiasm which needs no restraint. Under all other influences we must guard ourselves against yielding too completely, that thus we may live "soberly."

As to his fellowmen the believer lives "righteously." I cannot understand that Christian who can do a dirty thing in business. Craft, cunning, overreaching, misrepresentation, and deceit are no instruments for the hand of godly men. I am told that my principles are too angelic for business life—that a man cannot be a match for his fellowmen in trade, if he is too Puritanic. Others are up to tricks, and he will be ruined if he cannot trick them in return. O my dear hearers, do not talk in this way. If you mean to go the way of the devil, say so, and take the consequences; but if you profess to be servants of God, deny all partnership with unrighteousness. Dishonesty and falsehood are the opposites of godliness. A Christian man may be poor, but he must live righteously: he may lack sharpness, but he must not lack integrity. A Christian profession without uprightness is a lie. Grace must discipline us to righteous living.

Toward God we are told in the text that we are to be *godly*. Every man who has the grace of God in him indeed and of a truth will think much of God, and will seek first the kingdom of God and his righteousness. God will enter into all his calculations, God's presence will be his joy, God's strength will be his confidence, God's providence will be his inheritance, God's glory will be the chief end of his being, God's law the guide of his conversation. Now, if the grace of God, which has appeared so plainly to all men, has really come with its sacred discipline upon us, it is teaching us to live in this threefold manner.

Once more, there is looking, as well as living. One work of the grace of God is to cause us to be "looking for that blessed hope of the glorious appearing of the great God and our Savior Jesus Christ." What is that "blessed hope"? Why, first, that when he comes we shall rise from the dead, if we have fallen asleep; and that, if we are alive and remain, we shall be changed at his appearing. Our hope is that we shall be approved of him and shall hear him say, "Well done, good and faithful servant." This hope is not of debt, but of grace: though our Lord will give us a reward, it will not be according to the law of works. We expect to be like Jesus when we shall see him as he is. When Jesus shines forth as the sun, "then shall the righteous shine forth as the sun in the kingdom of our Father." Our gain by godliness cannot be counted down into the palm of our hand. It lies in the glorious future; and yet to faith it is so near that at this moment I almost hear the chariot of the coming One. The Lord comes, and in the coming of the Lord lies the great hope of the believer, his great stimulus to overcome evil, his incentive to perfect holiness in the fear of the Lord. Oh, to be found blameless in the day of the manifestation of our Lord! God grant us this! Do you not see, brethren, how the discipline of the doctrine of grace runs toward the separating of us from sin, and the making us to live unto God?

**3. Lastly, and briefly, the text sets forth certain of** *our encouragements*. **I will only briefly hint at them.**

In this great battle for right and truth and holiness, what could we do, my brethren and my sisters, if we were left alone? But our first encouragement is that grace has come to our rescue; for in the day when the Lord Jesus Christ appeared among men, he brought for us the grace of God to help us to overcome all iniquity. He that struggles now against inbred sin has the Holy Spirit within him to help him. He that goes forth to fight against evil in other men by preaching the gospel has that same Holy Ghost going with the truth to make it like a fire and like a hammer. I would ground my weapons, and retreat from a fight so hopeless were it not that the Lord of hosts is with us, the God of Jacob is our refuge. The grace of God that brings salvation from sin has flashed forth conspicuously like the lightning which is seen from one part of the heaven to the other, and our victory over darkness is insured. However hard the conflict with evil, it is not desperate. We may hope on and hope ever. A certain warrior was found in prayer, and when his king sneered, he answered that he was pleading with his majesty's august ally. I question whether God is the ally of anybody when he goes forth with gun and sword; but in using those weapons which are "not carnal, but mighty through God to the pulling down of strongholds," we may truly reckon upon our august ally. Speak the truth, man, for God speaks with you! Work for God, woman, for God works in you to will and to do of his own good pleasure. The appearance of the grace of God in the person of Christ is encouragement enough to those who are under the most difficult circumstances, and have to contend for righteousness against the deadliest odds. Grace has appeared; wherefore let us be of good courage!

A second encouragement is that another appearing is coming. He who bowed his head in weakness, and died in the moment of victory, is coming in all the glory of his endless life. Do not question it, the world is not going to darken into an eternal night: the morning comes as well as the night, and though sin and corruption abound, and the love of many waxes cold, these are but the tokens of his near advent who said that it would be so before his appearing. The right with the might and the might with the right shall be: as surely as God lives, it shall be so. We are not fighting a losing battle. The Lord must triumph. Oh, if his suffering life and cruel death had been the only appearing, we might have feared; but it is not: it is but the first, and the prefatory part of his manifestation. He comes! He comes! None can hinder his coming! Every moment brings him nearer; nothing can delay his glory. When the hour shall strike he shall appear in the majesty of God to put an end to the dominion of sin, and bring in endless peace. Satan shall be bruised under our feet shortly; wherefore comfort one another with these words, and then prepare for further battle. Grind your swords, and be ready for close fighting! Trust in God, and keep your powder dry. Ever this our war cry, "He must reign." We are looking for the appearing of the great God and Savior Jesus Christ.

Another encouragement is that we are serving a glorious Master. The Christ whom we follow is not a dead prophet like Muhammad. Truly we preach Christ crucified; but we also believe in Christ risen from the dead, in Christ gone up on high, in Christ soon to come a second time. He lives, and he lives as the great God and our Savior. If indeed you are soldiers of such a captain throw fear to the winds. Can you be cowards when the Lord of hosts leads you? Dare you tremble when at your head is the Wonderful, the Counselor, the mighty God, the everlasting Father, the Prince of peace? The trumpet is already at the lip of the archangel; who will not play the man? The great drum which makes the universe to throb, summons you to action.

> *Stand up, stand up for Jesus,*
> *Ye soldiers of the cross;*
> *Lift high his royal banner,*
> *It must not suffer loss.*

His cross is the old cross still, and none can overthrow it. Hallelujah, hallelujah to the name of Jesus!

Then come the tender thoughts with which I finish, the memories of what the Lord has done for us to make us holy: "Who gave himself for us." Special redemption, redemption with a wondrous price—"who gave himself for us." Put away that trumpet and that drum; take down the harp and gently touch its sweetest strings. Tell how the Lord Jesus loved us, and gave himself for us. O sirs, if nothing else can touch our hearts this must: "Ye are not your own, ye are bought with a price."

And he gave himself for us with these two objects: first, redemption, that he might redeem us from all iniquity; that he might break the bonds of sin asunder, and cast the cords of depravity far from us. He died—forget not that—died that your sins might die, died that every lust might be dragged into captivity at his chariot wheels. He gave himself for you that you might give yourselves for him.

Again, he died that he might purify us—purify us unto himself. How clean we must be if we are to be clean unto him. The holy Jesus will only commune with that which he has purified after the manner of his own nature; purified unto himself. He has purified us to be wholly his: no human hand may use the golden cup, no human incense may burn in the consecrated censer. We are purified unto himself, as the Hebrew would put it, to be his *segullah*, his peculiar possession. The translation "peculiar people" is unfortunate, because "peculiar" has come to mean odd, strange, singular. The passage really means that believers are Christ's own people, his choice and select portion. Saints are Christ's crown jewels, his box of diamonds; his very, very, very own. He carries his people as lambs in his bosom; he engraves their names on his heart. They are the inheritance to which he is the heir, and he values them more than all the universe beside. He would lose everything else sooner than lose one of them. He desires that you, who are being disciplined by his grace, should know that you are altogether his. You are Christ's men. You are each one to feel, "I do not belong to the world; I do not belong to myself; I belong only to Christ. I am set aside by him for himself only, and his I will be." The silver and the gold are his, and the cattle upon a thousand hills are his; but he makes small account of them, "the Lord's portion is his people."

The apostle finishes up by saying that we are to be a people "zealous of good works." Would to God that all Christian men and women were disciplined by divine grace till they became zealous for good works! In holiness zeal is sobriety. We are not only to approve of good works, and speak for good works, but we are to be red-hot for them. We are to be on fire for everything that is right and true. We may not be content to be quiet and inoffensive, but we are to be zealous of good works. Oh, that my Lord's grace would set us on fire in this way! There is plenty of fuel in the church, what is wanted is fire. A great many very respectable people are, in their sleepy way, doing as little as they can for any good cause. This will never do. We must wake up. Oh, the quantity of ambulance work that Christ's soldiers have to do! One half of Christ's army has to carry the other half. Oh, that our brethren could get off the sick list! Oh, that all of us were ardent, fervent, vigorous, zealous! Come, Holy Spirit, and quiet us! We may not go about to get this by our own efforts and energies, but God will work it by his grace. Grace given us in Christ is the fountainhead of all holy impulse. O heavenly grace, come like a flood at this time and bear us right away!

Oh, that those of you who have never felt the grace of God may be enabled to believe in the Lord Jesus Christ as to his first appearing! Then, trusting in his death upon the cross, you will learn to look for his second coming upon the throne, and you will rejoice therein. Unto his great name be glory forever and ever! Amen.

# The Watchword for Today: "Stand Fast"

Delivered on Lord's Day morning, April 17, 1887, at the Metropolitan Tabernacle, Newington. No. 1959.

> *For our conversation is in heaven, from whence also we look for the Savior, the Lord Jesus Christ: who shall change our vile body, that it may be fashioned like unto his glorious body, according to the working whereby he is able even to subdue all things unto himself. Therefore, my brethren dearly beloved and longed for, my joy and crown, so stand fast in the Lord, my dearly beloved.*
> —Philippians 3:20–4:1

Every doctrine of the Word of God has its practical bearing. As each tree bears seed after its kind, so does every truth of God bring forth practical virtues. Hence you find the apostle Paul very full of *therefores*—his therefores being the conclusions drawn from certain statements of divine truth. I marvel that our excellent translators should have divided the argument from the conclusion by making a new chapter where there is least reason for it.

Last Lord's Day I spoke with you concerning the most sure and certain resurrection of our Lord Jesus: now there is a practical force in that truth, which constitutes part of what is meant by "the power of his resurrection." Since the Lord has risen, and will surely come a second time, and will raise the bodies of his people at his coming, there is something to wait for, and a grand reason for steadfastness while thus waiting. We are looking for the coming of our Lord and Savior Jesus Christ from heaven, and that he shall "fashion anew the body of our humiliation, that it may be conformed to the body of his glory"; therefore let us stand fast in the position which will secure us this honor. Let us keep our posts until the coming of the great Captain shall release the sentinels. The glorious resurrection will abundantly repay us for all the toil and travail we may have to undergo in the battle for the Lord. The glory to be revealed even now casts a light upon our path, and causes sunshine within our hearts. The hope of this happiness makes us even now strong in the Lord, and in the power of his might.

Paul was deeply anxious that those in whom he had been the means of kindling the heavenly hope might be preserved faithful until the coming of Christ. He trembled lest any of them should seem to draw back, and prove traitors to their Lord. He dreaded lest he should lose what he hoped he had gained, by their turning aside from the faith. Hence he beseeches them to "stand fast." He expressed in the sixth verse of the first chapter his conviction that he who had begun a good work in them would perform it, but his intense love made him exhort them, saying, "Stand fast in the Lord, my dearly beloved." By such exhortations final perseverance is promoted and secured.

Paul has fought bravely; and in the case of the Philippian converts he believes that he has secured the victory, and he fears lest it should yet be lost. He reminds me of the death of that British hero, Wolfe, who on the heights of Quebec received a mortal wound. It was just at the moment when the enemy fled, and when he knew that they were running, a smile was on his face, and he cried, "Hold me up. Let not my brave soldiers see me drop. The day is ours. Oh, do keep it!" His sole anxiety was to make the victory sure. Thus warriors die, and thus Paul lived. His very soul seems to cry, "We have won the day. Oh, do keep it!" O my beloved hearers, I believe that many of you are "in the Lord," but I entreat you to "stand fast in the Lord." In your case, also, the day is won; but oh, do keep it! There is the pith of all I have to say to you this morning: may God the Holy Spirit write it on your hearts! Having done all things well thus far, I entreat you to obey the injunction of Jude, to "keep yourselves in the love of God," and to join with me in adoring him who alone is able to keep us from falling, and to present us faultless before his presence with exceeding great joy. Unto him be glory forever. Amen.

In leading out your thoughts I will keep to the following order:

First, it seems to me from the text that *the apostle perceived that these Philippian Christians were in their right place:* they were "in the Lord," and in such a position that he could safely bid them "stand fast" in it. Second, *he longed for them that they should keep their right place*—"Stand fast in the Lord, my dearly beloved"; and then, third, *he urged the best motives for their keeping their place.* These motives are contained in the first two verses of our text, upon which we will enlarge further on.

## 1. Paul joyfully perceived that *his beloved converts were in their right place.*

It is a very important thing indeed that we should begin well. The start is not everything, but it is a great deal. It has been said by the old proverb, that "well begun is half done"; and it is certainly so in the things of God. It is vitally important to enter in at the strait gate; to start on the heavenly journey from the right point. I have no doubt that many slips and falls and apostasies among professors are due to the fact that they were not right at first: the foundation was always upon the sand, and when the house came down at last, it was no more than might have been expected. A flaw in the foundation is pretty sure to be followed by a crack in the superstructure. Do see to it that you lay a good foundation. It is even better to have no repentance than a repentance which needs to be repented of: it is better to have no faith than a false faith: it is better to make no profession of religion than to make an untruthful one. God give us grace that we may not make a mistake in learning the alphabet of godliness, or else in all our learning we shall blunder on and increase in error. We should early learn the difference between grace and merit, between the purpose of God and the will of man, between trust in God and confidence in the flesh. If we do not start aright, the further we go the further we shall be from our desired end, and the more thoroughly in the wrong shall we find ourselves. Yes, it is of prime importance that our new birth and our first love should be genuine beyond all question.

The only position, however, in which we can begin aright is to be "in the Lord." This is to begin as we may safely go on. This is the essential point. It is a very good thing for Christians to be in the church; but if you are in the church before you are in the Lord you are out of place. It is a good thing to be engaged in holy work; but if you are in holy work before you are in the Lord you will have no heart for it, neither will the Lord accept it. It is not essential that you should be in this church or in that church; but it is essential that you should be "in the Lord"; it is not essential that you should be in the Sabbath school nor in the working meeting nor in the Tract Society; but it is essential to the last degree that you should be in the Lord. The apostle rejoiced over those that were converted at Philippi because he knew that they were in the Lord. They were where he wished them to remain, therefore he said, "Stand fast in the Lord."

What is it to be "in the Lord"? Well, brethren, *we are in the Lord vitally and evidently when we fly to the Lord Jesus by repentance and faith*, and make him to be our refuge and hiding place. Is it so with you? Have you fled out of self? Are you trusting in the Lord alone? Have you come to Calvary, and beheld your Savior? As the doves build their nests in the rock, have you thus made your home in Jesus? There is no shelter for a guilty soul but in his wounded side. Have you come there? Are you in him? Then keep there. You will never have a better refuge; in fact, there is no other. No other name is given under heaven among men whereby we must be saved. I cannot tell you to stand fast in the

Lord, unless you are there: hence my first inquiry is—Are you in Christ? Is he your only confidence? In his life, his death, and his resurrection do you find the grounds of your hope? Is he himself all your salvation, and all your desire? If so, stand fast in him.

Next, these people, in addition to having fled to Christ for refuge, were now *in Christ as to their daily life*. They had heard him say, "Abide in me"; and therefore they remained in the daily enjoyment of him, in reliance upon him, in obedience to him, and in the earnest copying of his example. They were Christians, that is to say, persons upon whom was named the name of Christ. They were endeavoring to realize the power of his death and resurrection as a sanctifying influence, killing their sins and fostering their virtues. They were laboring to reproduce his image in themselves, that so they might bring glory to his name. Their lives were spent within the circle of their Savior's influence. Are you so, my dear friends? Then stand fast. You will never find a nobler example; you will never be saturated with a diviner spirit than that of Christ Jesus your Lord. Whether we eat or drink, or whatsoever we do, let us do all in the name of the Lord Jesus, and so live in him.

These Philippians had, moreover, realized that they were *in Christ by a real and vital union with him*. They had come to feel, not like separated individualities, copying a model, but as members of a body made like to their head. By a living, loving, lasting union they were joined to Christ as their covenant head. They could say, "Who shall separate us from the love of God which is in Christ Jesus our Lord?" Do you know what it is to feel that the life which is in you is first in Christ, and still flows from him, even as the life of the branch is mainly in the stem? "I live; yet not I, but Christ liveth in me." This is to be in Christ. Are you in him in this sense? Forgive my pressing the question. If you answer me in the affirmative, I shall then entreat you to "stand fast" in him. It is in him, and in him only, that spiritual life is to be sustained, even as only from him can it be received. To be engrafted into Christ is salvation; but to abide in Christ is the full enjoyment of it. True union to Christ is eternal life. Paul, therefore, rejoiced over these Philippians, because they were joined unto the Lord in one spirit.

This expression is very short, but very full. "In Christ." Does it not mean that we are in Christ as the birds are in the air which buoys them up and enables them to fly? Are we not in Christ as the fish are in the sea? *Our Lord has become our element*, vital, and all surrounding. In him we live and move and have our being. He is in us, and we are in him. We are filled with all the fullness of God, because in Christ does all fullness dwell, and we dwell in him. Christ to us is all; he is in all; and he is all in all! Jesus to us is everything in everything. Without him we can *do* nothing, and we *are* nothing. Thus are we emphatically in him. If you have reached this point, "stand fast" in it. If you dwell in the secret place of the tabernacles of the most High, abide under the shadow of the Almighty. Do you sit at his table, and eat of his dainties? Then prolong the visit, and think not of removal. Say in your soul—

> *Here would I find a settled rest,*
> *While others go and come;*
> *No more a stranger, or a guest,*
> *But like a child at home.*

Has Jesus brought you into his green pastures? Then lie down in them. Go no further, for you will never fare better. Stay with your Lord, however long the night, for only in him have you hope of morning.

You see, then, that these people were where they should be—in the Lord, and that this was the reason why the apostle took such delight in them. Kindly read the first verse of the fourth chapter, and see how he loves them, and joys over them. He heaps up titles of love! Some dip their morsel in vinegar, but Paul's words were saturated with honey. Here we not only have sweet words, but they mean something: his love was real and fervent. The very heart of Paul is written out large in this verse—"Therefore, my brethren dearly beloved and longed for, my joy and crown, so stand fast in the Lord, my dearly beloved." Because they were in Christ, therefore first of all they were Paul's *brethren*. This was a new relationship, not earthly, but heavenly. What did this Jew from Tarsus know about the Philippians? Many of them were Gentiles. Time was when he would have called them dogs, and despised them as the uncircumcised; but now he says, "my brethren." That poor word has become very hackneyed. We talk of brethren without particularly much of brotherly love, but true brothers have a love for one another which is very unselfish and admirable, and so there is between real Christians a brotherhood which they will neither disown nor dissemble nor forget. It is said of our Lord, "For this cause he is not ashamed to call them brethren"; and surely they need never be ashamed to call one another brethren. Paul, at any rate, looks at the jailer, that jailor who had set his feet in the stocks, and he looks at the jailer's family, and at Lydia, and many others; in fact, at the whole company that he had gathered at Philippi, and he salutes them lovingly as "my brethren." Their names were written in the same family register, because they were in Christ and therefore had one Father in heaven.

Next, the apostle calls them "my *dearly beloved.*" The verse almost begins with this word, and it quite finishes with it. The repetition makes it mean, "my doubly dear ones." Such is the love which every true servant of Christ will have for those who have been begotten to the faith of Christ by his means. Oh yes, if you are in Christ his ministers must love you. How could there be a lack of affection in our hearts toward you, since we have been the means of bringing you to Jesus? Without cant or display we call you our "dearly beloved."

Then the apostle calls them his *"longed for,"* that is, his most desired ones. He first desired to see them converted; after that he desired to see them baptized; then he desired to see them exhibiting all the graces of Christians. When he saw holiness in them, he desired to visit them and commune with them. Their constant kindness created in him a strong desire to speak with them face to face. He loved them, and desired their company, because they were in Christ. So he speaks of them as those for whom he longed. His delight was in thinking of them and in hoping to visit them.

Then he adds, "my joy and crown." Paul had been the means of their salvation, and when he thought of that blessed result he never regretted all that he had suffered: his persecutions among the Gentiles seemed light indeed since these priceless souls were his reward. Though he was nothing but a poor prisoner of Christ, yet he talks in right royal style: they are his crown. They were his *stephanos*, or crown given as a reward for his life race. This among the Greeks was usually a wreath of flowers placed around the victor's brow. Paul's crown would never fade. He writes as he felt the amaranth around his temples: even now he looks upon the Philippians as his chaplet of honor: they were his joy and his crown; he anticipated, I do not doubt, that throughout eternity it would be a part of his heaven to see them amid their blessedness, and to know that he helped to bring them to that felicity by leading them to Christ. O beloved, it is indeed our highest joy that we have not run in vain, neither labored in vain: you who have been snatched as "brands from the burning," and are now living to the praise of our Lord Jesus Christ, you are our prize, our crown, our joy.

These converts were all this to Paul simply because they were "in Christ." They had begun well, they were where they should be, and he, therefore, rejoiced in them.

2. But second, it was for this reason that *he longed that they should keep there.*

He entreated them to stand fast. "So stand fast in the Lord, my dearly beloved." The beginning of religion is not the whole of it. You must not suppose that the sum of godliness is contained within the experience of a day or two or a week or a few months or even a few years. Precious are the feelings which attend conversion; but dream not that repentance, faith, and so forth, are for a season, and then all is done and done with. I am afraid there are some who secretly say, "Everything is now complete; I have experienced the necessary change, I have been to see the elders and the pastor, and I have been baptized, and received into the church, and now all is right forever." That is a false view of your condition. In conversion you have started in the race, and you must run to the end of the course. In your confession of Christ, you have carried your tools into the vineyard, but the day's work now begins. Remember, "He that shall endure unto the end, the same shall be saved." Godliness is a lifelong business. The working out of the salvation which the Lord himself works in you is not a matter of certain hours, and of a limited period of life. Salvation is unfolded throughout all our sojourn here. We continue to repent and to believe, and even the process of our conversion continues as we are changed more and more into the image of our Lord. Final perseverance is the necessary evidence of genuine conversion.

In proportion as we rejoice over converts, we feel an intense bitterness when any disappoint us, and turn out to be merely temporary camp followers. We sigh over the seed which sprang up so speedily, but which withers so soon because it has neither root nor depth of earth. We were ready to say, "Ring the bells of heaven"; but the bells of heaven did not ring because these people talked about Christ, and said they were in Christ; but it was all a delusion. After a while, for one reason and another, they went back; "they went out from us, but they were not of us; for if they had been of us, they would no doubt have continued with us: but they went out, that they might be made manifest that they were not all of us." Our churches suffer most seriously from the great numbers who drop out of their ranks, and either go back to the world, or else must be pursuing a very secret and solitary path in their way to heaven, for we hear no more of them. Our joy is turned to disappointment, our crown of laurel becomes a circle of faded leaves, and we are weary at the remembrance of it. With what earnestness, therefore, would we say to you who are beginning the race, "Continue in your course. We beseech you turn not aside, neither slacken your running, till you have won the prize"!

I heard an expression yesterday which pleased me much. I spoke about the difficulty of keeping on. "Yes," answered my friend, "and it is harder still to keep on keeping on." So it is. There is the pinch. I know lots of fellows who are wonders at the start. What a rush they make! But then there is no stay in them; they soon lose breath. The difference between the spurious and the real Christian lies in this staying power. The real Christian has a life within him which can never die, an incorruptible seed which lives and abides forever; but the spurious Christian begins after a fashion, but ends almost as soon as he begins. He is esteemed a saint; but turns out a hypocrite. He makes a fair show for a while, but soon he quits the way of holiness, and makes his own damnation sure. God save you, dear friends, from anything which looks like apostasy. Hence I would with all my might press upon you these two most weighty words: "Stand fast."

I will put the exhortation thus: "Stand fast *doctrinally*." In this age all the ships in the waters are pulling up their anchors: they are drifting with the tide; they are driven about with every wind. It is your wisdom to put down more anchors. I have taken the precaution to cast four anchors out of the stern, as well as to see that the great bower anchor is in its proper place. I will not budge an inch from the old doctrine for any man. Now that the cyclone is triumphant over many a bowing wall and tottering fence, those who are built upon the one foundation must prove its value by standing fast. We will hearken to no teaching but that of the Lord Jesus. If you see a truth to be in God's Word, grasp it by your faith; and if it be unpopular, grapple it to you as with hooks of steel. If you are despised as a fool for holding it, hold it the more. Like an oak, take deeper root, because the winds would tear you from your place. Defy reproach and ridicule, and you have already vanquished it. Stand fast, like the British squares in the olden times. When fierce assaults were made upon them, every man seemed transformed to rock. We might have wandered from the ranks a little in more peaceful times, to look after the fascinating flowers which grow on every side of our march; but now we know that the enemy surrounds us, we keep strictly to the line of march, and tolerate no roaming. The watchword of the host of God just now is "Stand fast!" Hold you to the faith once delivered to the saints. Hold fast the form of sound words, and deviate not one jot or tittle therefrom. Doctrinally stand fast!

*Practically*, also, abide firm in the right, the true, the holy. This is of the utmost importance. The barriers are broken down; they would amalgamate church and world: yes, even church and stage. It is proposed to combine God and devil in one service; Christ and Belial are to perform on one stage. Surely now is the time when the lion shall eat straw like the ox, and very dirty straw too. So they say; but I repeat to you this word, "Come out from among them, and be ye separate, and touch not the unclean thing." Write "holiness unto the Lord" not only on your altars, but upon the bells of the horses; let everything be done as before the living God. Do all things unto holiness and edification. Strive together to maintain the purity of the disciples of Christ; and take up your cross, and go without the camp bearing his reproach. If you have already stood apart in your decision for the Lord, continue to do so. Stand fast. In nothing moved by the laxity of the age, in nothing affected by the current of modern opinion, say to yourself, "I will do as Christ bids me to the utmost of my ability. I will follow the Lamb whithersoever he goes." In these times of worldliness, impurity, self-indulgence, and error, it becomes the Christian to gather up his skirts and keep his feet and his garments clean from the pollution which lies all around him. We must be more Puritanic and precise than we have been. Oh, for grace to stand fast!

Mind also that you stand fast *experimentally*. Pray that your inward experience may be a close adhesion to your Master. Do not go astray from his presence. Neither climb with those who dream of perfection in the flesh, nor grovel with those who doubt the possibility of present salvation. Take the Lord Jesus Christ to be your sole treasure, and let your heart be ever with him. Stand fast in faith in his atonement, in confidence in his divinity, in assurance of his second advent. I pine to know within my soul the power of his resurrection, and to have unbroken fellowship with him. In communion with the Father and the Son let us stand fast. He shall fare well whose heart and soul, affections and understanding are wrapped up in Christ Jesus, and in none beside. Concerning your inward life, your secret prayer, your walk with God, here is the watchword of the day: "Stand fast."

To put it very plainly, "Stand fast *in the Lord," without wishing for another trust*. Do not desire to have any hope but that which is in Christ. Do not entertain the proposition that you should unite another confidence to your confidence in the Lord. Have no hankering after any other fashion of faith except the faith of a sinner in his Savior. All hope but that which is set before us in the gospel and brought to us by the Lord Jesus is a poisoned delicacy, highly colored, but by no means to be so much as tasted by those who have been fed upon the bread of heaven. What need we more than Jesus? What way of salvation do we seek but that of grace? What security but the precious blood? Stand fast; and wish for no other rock of salvation save the Lord Jesus.

Next, stand fast *without wavering in our trust*. Permit no doubt to worry you. Know that Jesus can save you, and, what is more, know that he has saved you. So commit yourself to his hands, that you are as sure of your salvation as of your existence. The blood of Jesus Christ this day cleanses us from all sin; his righteousness covers us, and his life quickens us into newness of life. Tolerate no doubt, mistrust, suspicion, or misgiving. Believe in Christ up to the hilt. All for myself, I will yield to be lost forever if Jesus does not save me. I will have no other string to my bow, no second door of hope, or way of retreat. I could risk a thousand souls on my Lord's truth and feel no risk. Stand fast, without wishing for another trust, and without wavering in the trust you have.

Moreover, stand fast *without wandering into sin*. You are tempted this way and that way: stand fast. Inward passions rise; lusts of the flesh rebel, the devil hurls his fearful suggestions; the men of your own household tempt you: stand fast. Only so will you be preserved from the torrents of iniquity. Keep close to the example and spirit of your Master; and having done all, still stand.

As I have said, stand fast without wandering, so next I must say stand fast *without wearying*. You are a little tired. Never mind, take a little rest and brush up again. "Oh," you say, "this toil is so monotonous." Do it better, and that will be a change. Your Savior endured his life and labor without this complaint, for zeal had eaten him up. "Alas!" you cry, "I cannot see results." Never mind; wait for results, even as the husbandman waits for the precious fruits of the earth. "Oh, sir, I plod along and make no progress." Never mind, you are a poor judge of your own success. Work on, for in due season you shall reap if you faint not. Practice perseverance. Remember that if you have the work of faith and the labor of love, you must complete the trio by adding the patience of hope. You cannot do without this last. "Be ye steadfast, unmovable, always abounding in the work of the Lord, forasmuch as ye know that your labor is not in vain in the Lord." I am reminded of Sir Christopher Wren, when he cleared away old St. Paul's to make room for his splendid pile. He was compelled to use battering rams upon the massive walls. The workmen kept on battering and battering. An enormous force was brought to bear upon the walls for days and nights, but it did not appear to have made the least impression upon the ancient masonry. Yet the great architect knew what he was at: he bade them keep on incessantly, and the ram fell again and again upon the rocky wall, till at length the whole mass was disintegrating and coming apart; and then each stroke began to tell. At a blow it reeled, at another it quivered, at another it moved visibly, at another it fell over amid clouds of dust. These last strokes did the work. Do you think so? No, it was the combination of blows, the first as truly as the last. Keep on with the battering ram. I hope to keep on until I die. And, mark you, I may die and I may not see the errors of the hour totter to their fall, but I shall be perfectly content to sleep in Christ, for I have a sure expectation that this work will succeed in the end. I shall be happy to have done my share of the work, even if I personally see little apparent result. Lord, let your work appear unto your servants, and we will be content that your glory should be reserved for our children. Stand fast, my brethren, in incessant labors, for the end is sure.

And then, in addition to standing fast in that respect, stand fast *without warping*. Timber, when it is rather green, is apt to go this way or that. The spiritual weather is very bad just now for green wood: it is one day damp with superstition, and another day it is parched with skepticism. Rationalism and ritualism are both at work. I pray that you may not warp. Keep straight; keep to the truth, the whole truth, and nothing but the truth; for in the Master's name we bid you "Stand fast in the Lord."

Stand fast, for there is great need. Many walk of whom I have told you often, and now tell you even weeping, that they are the enemies of the cross of Christ.

Paul urged them to stand fast because, even in his own case, spiritual life was a struggle. Even Paul said, "Not as though I had already attained." He was pressing forward; he was straining his whole energy by the power of the Holy Ghost. He did not expect to be carried to heaven on a featherbed; he was warring and agonizing. You, beloved, must do the same. What a grand example of perseverance did Paul set to us all! Nothing enticed him from his steadfastness. "None of these things move me," said he, "neither count I my life dear unto me." He has entered into his rest, because the Lord his God helped him to stand fast, even to the end. I wish I had power to put this more earnestly, but my very soul goes forth with it. "Stand fast in the Lord, my dearly beloved."

### 3. Third, *the apostle urged the best motives for their standing fast.*

He says, "Stand fast *because of your citizenship.*" Read the twentieth verse: "For our citizenship is in heaven." Now, if you are what you profess to be, if you are in Christ, you are citizens of the New Jerusalem. Men ought to behave themselves according to their citizenship, and not dishonor their city. When a man was a citizen of Athens, in the olden time, he felt it incumbent upon him to be brave. Xerxes said, "These Athenians are not ruled by kings: how will they fight?" "No," said one, "but every man respects the law, and each man is ready to die for his country." Xerxes soon had to know that the like obedience and respect of law ruled the Spartans, and that these, because they were of Sparta, were all brave as lions. He sends word to Leonidas and his little troop to give up their arms. "Come and take them," was the courageous reply. The Persian king had myriads of soldiers with him, while Leonidas had only three hundred Spartans at his side; yet they kept the pass, and it cost the eastern despot many thousands of men to force a passage. The sons of Sparta died rather than desert their post. Every citizen of Sparta felt that he must stand fast: it was not for such a man as he to yield. I like the spirit of Bayard, that "knight without fear and without reproach." He knew not what fear meant. In his last battle, his spine was broken, and he said to those around him, "Place me up against a tree, so that I may sit up and die with my face to the enemy." Yes, if our backs were broken, if we could no more bear the shield or use the sword, it would be incumbent upon us, as citizens of the New Jerusalem, to die with our faces toward the enemy. We must not yield, we dare not yield, if we are of the city of the great King. The martyrs cry to us to stand fast; the cloud of witnesses bending from their thrones above beseech us to stand fast; yes, all the hosts of the shining ones cry to us, "Stand fast." Stand fast for God, and the truth, and holiness, and let no man take your crown.

The next argument that Paul used was *their outlook*. "Our conversation is in heaven; from whence also we look for the Savior, the Lord Jesus Christ." Brethren, Jesus is coming. He is even now on the way. You have heard our tidings till you scarcely credit us; but the word is true, and it will surely be fulfilled before long. The Lord is coming indeed. He promised to come to die, and he kept his word: he now promises to come to reign, and be you sure that he will keep his tryst with his people. He is coming. Ears of faith can hear the sound of his chariot wheels; every moment of time, every event of providence is bringing him nearer. Blessed are those servants who shall not be sleeping when he comes nor wandering from their posts of duty; happy shall they be whom their Lord shall find faithfully watching and standing fast in that great day!

To us, beloved, he is coming, not as Judge and destroyer, but as *Savior*. We look for the Savior, the Lord Jesus Christ. Now, if we do look for him, let us "stand fast." There must be no going into sin, no forsaking the fellowship of the church, no leaving the truth, no trying to play fast and loose with godliness, no running with the hare and hunting with the hounds. Let us stand so fast in singleness of heart that, whenever Jesus comes, we shall be able to say, "Welcome, welcome, Son of God!"

Sometimes I wait through the weary years with great comfort. There was a ship some time ago outside a certain harbor. A heavy sea made the ship roll fearfully. A dense fog blotted out all buoys and lights. The captain never left the wheel. He could not tell his way into the harbor, and no pilot could get out to him for a long time. Eager passengers urged him to be courageous and make a dash for the harbor. He said, "No; it is not my duty to run so great a risk. A pilot is required here, and I will wait for one if I wait a week." The truest courage is that which can bear to be charged with cowardice. To wait is much wiser than when you cannot hear the foghorn and have no pilot yet to steam on and wreck your vessel on the rocks. Our prudent captain waited his time, and at last he espied the pilot's boat coming to him over the boiling sea.

When the pilot was at his work the captain's anxious waiting was over. The church is like that vessel, she is pitched to and fro in the storm and the dark, and the pilot has not yet come. The weather is very threatening. All around the darkness hangs like a pall. But Jesus will come, walking on the water, before long; he will bring us safe to the desired haven. Let us wait with patience. Stand fast! Stand fast! for Jesus is coming, and in him is our sure hope.

Further, there was another motive. *There was an expectation.* "He shall change our vile body," or rather, "body of our humiliation." Only think of it, dear friends! No more headaches or heartaches, no more feebleness and fainting, no more inward tumor or consumption; but the Lord shall transfigure this body of our humiliation into the likeness of the body of his glory. Our frame is now made up of decaying substances, it is of the earth earthy. "So to the dust return we must." This body groans, suffers, becomes diseased, and dies: blessed be God, it shall be wonderfully changed, and then there shall be no more death, neither sorrow nor crying, neither shall there be any more pain. The natural appetites of this body engender sad tendencies to sin, and in this respect it is a "vile body." It shall not always be so; the great change will deliver it from all that is gross and carnal. It shall be pure as the Lord's body! Whatever the body of Christ is now, our body is to be like it. We spoke of it last Sunday, you know, when we heard him say, "Handle me." We are to have a real, corporeal body as he had for substance and reality; and, like his body, it will be full of beauty, full of health and strength; it will enjoy peculiar immunities from evil, and special adaptations for good. That is what is going to happen to me and to you; therefore let us stand fast. Let us not willfully throw away our prospects of glory and immortality. What! Relinquish resurrection? Relinquish glory? Relinquish likeness to the risen Lord? O God, save us from such a terrible piece of apostasy! Save us from such immeasurable folly! Suffer us not to turn our backs in the day of battle, since that would be to turn our backs from the crown of life that fades not away.

Last, the apostle urges us to stand fast because of *our resources*. Somebody may ask, "How can this body of yours be transformed and transfigured until it becomes like the body of Christ?" I cannot tell you anything about the process; it will all be accomplished in the twinkling of an eye, at the last trump. But I can tell you by what power it will be accomplished. The omnipotent Lord will lay bare his arm and exercise his might, "according to the working whereby he is able even to subdue all things unto himself." O brethren, we may well stand fast since we have infinite power at our backs. The Lord is with us with all his energy, even with his all-conquering strength, which shall yet subdue all his foes. Do not let us imagine that any enemy can be too strong for Christ's arm. If he is able to subdue all things unto himself, he can certainly bear us through all opposition. One glance of his eye may wither all opposers, or, better still, one word from his lips may turn them into friends. The army of the Lord is strong in reserves. These reserves have never yet been fully called out. We, who are in the field, are only a small squadron, holding the fort; but our Lord has at his back ten thousand times ten thousand who will carry war into the enemy's camp. When the Captain of our salvation comes to the front, he will bring his heavenly legions with him. Our business is to watch until he appears upon the scene, for when he comes, his infinite resources will be put in marching order. I like that speech of Wellington (who was so calm amid the roar of Waterloo), when an officer sent word, "Tell the commander in chief that he must move me, I cannot hold my position any longer, my numbers are so thinned." "Tell him," said the great general, "he *must* hold his place. Every Englishman today must die where he stands, or else win the victory." The officer read the command to stand, and he did stand till the trumpet sounded victory. And so it is now. My brethren, we must die where we are rather than yield to the enemy. If Jesus tarries we must not desert our posts. Wellington knew that the heads of the Prussian columns would soon be visible, coming in to ensure the victory; and so by faith we can perceive the legions of our Lord approaching: in serried ranks his angels fly through the opening heaven. The air is teeming with them. I hear their silver trumpets. Behold, he comes with clouds! When he comes he will abundantly recompense all who stood fast amid the rage of battle. Let us sing, "Hold the fort, for I am coming."

# "He Cometh with Clouds"

~~~

Delivered at the Metropolitan Tabernacle, Newington. No. 1989.

*Behold, he cometh with clouds; and every eye shall see him, and they also which pierced him: and all kindreds of the earth shall wail because of him. Even so, Amen.* —REVELATION 1:7

In reading the chapter we observed how the beloved John saluted the seven churches in Asia with, "Grace and peace be unto you." Blessed men scatter blessings. When the *benediction* of God rests on us we pour out benedictions upon others.

From benediction John's gracious heart rose into *adoration* of the great King of saints. As our hymn puts it, "The holy to the holiest leads." They that are good at blessing men will be quick at blessing God.

It is a wonderful doxology which John has given us: "Unto him that loved us, and washed us from our sins in his own blood, and hath made us kings and priests unto God and his Father; to him be glory and dominion forever and ever. Amen." I like the Revised Version for its alliteration in this case, although I cannot prefer it for other reasons. It runs thus: "Unto him that *loveth* us, and *loosed* us from our sins by his blood." Truly our Redeemer has loosed us from sin; but the mention of his blood suggests washing rather than loosing. We can keep the alliteration and yet retain the meaning of cleansing if we read the passage, "Unto him that loved us, and laved us." *Loved* us, and *laved* us: carry those two words home with you: let them lie upon your tongue to sweeten your breath for prayer and praise. "Unto him that loved us, and laved us, be glory and dominion forever and ever."

Then John tells of the dignity which the Lord has put upon us in making us kings and priests, and from this he ascribes royalty and dominion unto the Lord himself. John had been extolling the great King, whom he calls, "the Prince of the kings of the earth." Such indeed he was, and is, and is to be. When John had touched upon that royalty which is natural to our divine Lord, and that dominion which has come to him by conquest, and by the gift of the Father as the reward of all his travail, he then went on to note that he has "made us kings." Our Lord's royalty he diffuses among his redeemed. We praise him because he is in himself a king, and next, because he is a king maker, the fountain of honor and majesty. He has not only enough of royalty for himself, but he hands a measure of his dignity to his people. He makes kings out of such common stuff as he finds in us poor sinners. Shall we not adore him for this? Shall we not cast our crowns at his feet? He gave our crowns to us, shall we not give them to him? "To him be glory and dominion forever and ever. Amen." King by thy divine nature! King by filial right! King maker, lifting up the beggar from the dunghill to set him among princes! King of kings by the unanimous love of all your crowned ones! you are he whom your brethren shall praise! Reign forever and ever! Unto you be hosannas of welcome and hallelujahs of praise. Lord of the earth and heaven, let all things that be, or ever shall be, render unto you all glory in the highest degree. Brethren, do not your souls take fire as you think of the praises of Emmanuel? Fain would I fill the universe with his praise. Oh, for a thousand tongues to sing the glories of the Lord Jesus! If the Spirit who dictated the words of John has taken possession of our spirits, we shall find adoration to be our highest delight. Never are we so near to heaven as when we are absorbed in the worship of Jesus, our Lord and God. Oh, that I could now adore him as I shall do when, delivered from this encumbering body, my soul shall behold him in the fullness of his glory!

It would seem from the chapter that the adoration of John was increased by his expectation of the Lord's second coming; for he cries, "Behold, he cometh with clouds." His adoration awoke his expectation, which all the while was lying in his soul as an element of that vehement heat of reverent love which he poured forth in his doxology. "Behold, he cometh," said he, and thus he revealed one source of his reverence. "Behold, he cometh," said he, and this exclamation was the result of his reverence. He adored until his faith realized his Lord and became a second and nobler sight.

I think, too, that his reverence was deepened and his adoration was rendered more fervent by his conviction of the speediness of his Lord's coming. "Behold, he cometh" or is coming: he means to assert that he is even now on his way. As workmen are moved to be more diligent in service when they hear their master's footfall, so, doubtless, saints are quickened in their devotion when they are conscious that he whom they worship is drawing near. He has gone away to the Father for a while, and so he has left us alone in this world; but he has said, "I will come again and receive you unto myself," and we are confident that he will keep his word. Sweet is the remembrance of that loving promise. That assurance is pouring its savor into John's heart while he is adoring; and it becomes inevitable, as well as most meet and proper, that his doxology should at its close introduce him to the Lord himself, and cause him to cry out, "Behold, he cometh." Having worshiped among the pure in heart, he sees the Lord: having adored the King, he sees him assume the judgment seat, and appear in the clouds of heaven. When once we enter upon heavenly things, we know not how far we can go nor how high we can climb. John who began with blessing the churches now beholds his Lord.

May the Holy Ghost help us reverently to think of the wondrous coming of our blessed Lord, when he shall appear to the delight of his people and the dismay of the ungodly!

There are three things in the text. They will seem commonplace to some of you, and, indeed, they are the commonplace of our divine faith, and yet nothing can be of greater importance. The first is, *our Lord Jesus comes*: "Behold, he cometh with clouds." The second is, *our Lord Jesus Christ's coming will be seen of all*: "Every eye shall see him, and they also which pierced him." And, in the third place, *this coming will cause great sorrow*: "All kindreds of the earth shall wail because of him."

## 1. May the Holy Spirit help us while, in the first place, we remember that *our Lord Jesus Christ comes*!

This announcement is thought worthy of a note of admiration. As the Latins would say, there is an *Ecce* placed here: "Behold, he cometh." As in the old books the printers put hands in the margin pointing to special passages, such is this "Behold!" It is a *nota bene* calling upon us to note well what we are reading. Here is something which we are to *hold* and *behold*. We now hear a voice crying, "Come and see!" The Holy Spirit never uses superfluous words, nor redundant notes of exclamation; when he cries, "Behold!," it is because there is reason for deep and lasting attention. Will you turn away when he bids you pause and ponder, linger, and look? O you that have been beholding vanity, come and behold the fact that Jesus comes. You that have been beholding this, and beholding that, and thinking of nothing worthy of your thoughts; forget these passing sights and spectacles, and for once behold a scene which has no parallel. It is not a monarch in her jubilee, but the King of kings in his glory. That same Jesus who went up from Olivet into heaven is coming again to earth in like manner as his disciples saw him go up into heaven. Come and behold this great sight. If ever there was a thing in the world worth looking at, it is this. Behold and see if there was ever glory like unto his glory! Hearken to the midnight cry, "Behold, the bridegroom cometh!" It has practically to do with you. "Go ye forth to meet him." This voice is to you, O sons of men. Do not carelessly turn aside; for the Lord God himself demands your attention: he commands you to "Behold!" Will you be blind when God bids you behold? Will you shut your eyes when your Savior cries, "Behold"? When the finger of inspiration points the way, will not your eye follow where it directs you? "Behold, he cometh." O my hearers, look hither, I beseech you.

If we read the words of our text carefully, this "Behold" shows us first, that this coming is to be vividly realized. I think I see John. He is in the spirit; but on a sudden he seems startled into a keener and more solemn attention. His mind is more awake than usual, though he was ever a man of bright eyes that saw afar. We always liken him to the eagle for the height of his fight and the keenness of his vision; yet on a sudden, even he seems startled with a more astounding vision. He cries out, "Behold! Behold!" He has caught sight of his Lord. He says not, "He will come by and by," but, "I can see him; he is now coming." He has evidently realized the second advent. He has so conceived of the second coming of the Lord that it has become a matter of fact to him; a matter to be spoken of and even to be written down. "Behold, he cometh!" Have you and I ever realized the coming of Christ so fully as this? Perhaps we believe that he will come. I should hope that we all do that. If we believe that the Lord Jesus has come the first time, we believe also that he will come the second time; but are these equally assured truths to us? Peradventure we have vividly realized the first appearing: from Bethlehem to Golgotha, and from Calvary to Olivet we have traced the Lord, understanding that blessed cry, "Behold the Lamb of God, which taketh away the sin of the world!" Yes, the Word was made flesh and dwelt among us, and we beheld his glory, the glory as of the only begotten of the Father, full of grace and truth. But have we with equal firmness grasped the thought that he comes again without a sin offering unto salvation? Do we now say to each other, as we meet in happy fellowship, "Yes, our Lord comes"? It should be to us not only a prophecy assuredly believed among us, but a scene pictured in our souls, and anticipated in our hearts. My imagination has often set forth that dread scene: but better still, my faith has realized it. I have heard the chariot wheels of the Lord's approach, and I have endeavored to set my house in order for his reception. I have felt the shadow of that great cloud which shall attend him, damping the ardor of my worldliness. I hear even now in spirit the sound of the last trumpet, whose tremendous blast startles my soul to serious action and puts force into my life. Would God that I lived more completely under the influence of that august event!

Brothers and sisters, to this realization I invite you. I wish that we could go together in this, until as we went out of the house we said to one another, "Behold, he cometh!" One said to his fellow, after the Lord had risen, "The Lord has risen indeed." I want you tonight to feel just as certain that the Lord is coming indeed, and I would have you say as much to one another. We are sure that he will come, and that he is on the way; but the benefit of a more vivid realization would be incalculable.

*This coming is to be zealously proclaimed*, for John does not merely calmly say, "He cometh," but he vigorously cries, "Behold, he cometh." Just as the herald of a king prefaces his message by a trumpet blast that calls attention, so John cries, "Behold!" As the old town crier was inclined to say, "Oh yes! Oh yes! Oh yes!" or to use some other striking formula by which he called upon men to note his announcement, so John stands in the midst of us, and cries, "Behold, he cometh!" He calls attention by that emphatic word "behold." It is no ordinary message that he brings, and he would not have us treat his word as a commonplace saying. He throws his heart into the announcement. He proclaims it loudly, he proclaims it solemnly, and he proclaims it with authority: "Behold, he cometh."

Brethren, no truth ought to be more frequently proclaimed, next to the first coming of the Lord, than his second coming; and you cannot thoroughly set forth all the ends and bearings of the first advent if you forget the second. At the Lord's Supper, there is no discerning the Lord's body unless you discern his first coming; but there is no drinking into his cup to its fullness, unless you hear him say, "Until I come." You must look forward, as well as backward. So must it be with all our ministries; they must look to him on the cross and on the throne. We must vividly realize that he, who has once come, is coming yet again, or else our testimony will be marred, and one-sided. We shall make lame work of preaching and teaching if we leave out either advent.

And next, *it is to be unquestionably asserted*. "Behold, he cometh." It is not, "Perhaps he will come"; nor, "Perhaps he may yet appear." "Behold, he cometh" should be dogmatically asserted as an absolute certainty, which has been realized by the heart of the man who proclaims it. "Behold, he cometh." All the prophets say that he will come. From Enoch down to the last that spoke by inspiration, they declare, "The Lord cometh with ten thousands of his saints." You shall not find one who has spoken by the authority of God, who does not, either directly or by implication, assert the coming of the Son of man, when the multitudes born of woman shall be summoned to his bar, to receive the recompense of their deeds. All the promises are travailing with this prognostication, "Behold, he cometh." We have his own word for it, and this makes assurance doubly sure. He has told us that he will come again. He often assured his disciples that if he went away from them, he would come again to them; and he left us the Lord's Supper as a parting token to be observed until he comes. As often as we break bread we are reminded of the fact that, though it is a most blessed ordinance, yet it is a temporary one, and will cease to be celebrated when our absent Lord is once again present with us.

What, dear brethren, is there to hinder Christ from coming? When I have studied and thought over this word, "Behold, he cometh," yes, I have said to myself, indeed he does; who shall hold him back? His heart is with his church on earth. In the place where he fought the battle he desires to celebrate the victory. His delights are with the sons of men. All his saints are waiting for the day of his appearing, and he is waiting also. The very earth in her sorrow and her groaning travails for his coming, which is to be her redemption. The creation is made subject to vanity for a little while; but when the Lord shall come again, the creation itself also shall be delivered from the bondage of corruption into the glorious liberty of the children of God. We might question whether he would come a second time if he had not already come the first time; but if he came to Bethlehem, be assured that his feet shall yet stand upon Olivet. If he came to die, doubt not that he will come to reign. If he came to be despised and rejected of men, why should we doubt that he will come to be admired in all them that believe? His sure coming is to be unquestionably asserted.

Dear friends, this fact that he will come again, *is to be taught as demanding our immediate interest.* "Behold, he cometh with clouds." Behold, look at it; meditate on it. It is worth thinking of. It concerns yourself. Study it again and again. "He cometh." He will so soon be here that it is put in the present tense: "He cometh." That shaking of the earth; that blotting out of sun and moon; that fleeing of heaven and earth before his face—all these are so nearly here that John describes them as accomplished. "Behold, he cometh."

There is this sense lying in the background—that *he is already on the way.* All that he is doing in providence and grace is a preparation for his coming. All the events of human history, all the great decisions of his august majesty whereby he rules all things—all these are tending toward the day of his appearing. Do not think that he delays his coming, and then upon a sudden he will rush hither in hot haste. He has arranged for it to take place as soon as wisdom allows. We know not what may make the present delay imperative; but the Lord knows, and that suffices. You grow uneasy because nearly two thousand years have passed since his ascension, and Jesus has not yet come; but you do not know what had to be arranged for, and how far the lapse of time was absolutely necessary for the Lord's designs. Those are no little matters which have filled up the great pause: the intervening centuries have teemed with wonders. A thousand things may have been necessary in heaven itself before the consummation of all things could be arrived at. When our Lord comes it shall be seen that he came as quickly as he could, speaking after the manner of his infinite wisdom; for he cannot behave himself otherwise than wisely, perfectly, divinely. He cannot be moved by fear or passion so as to act hastily as you and I too often do. He dwells in the leisure of eternity, and in the serenity of omnipotence. He has not to measure out days, and months, and years, and to accomplish so much in such a space or else leave his lifework undone; but according to the power of an endless life he proceeds steadily on, and to him a thousand years are but as one day. Therefore be assured that the Lord is even now coming. He is making everything tend that way. All things are working toward that grand climax. At this moment, and every moment since he went away, the Lord Jesus has been coming back again. "Behold, he cometh!" He is on the way! He is nearer every hour! And we are told that *his coming will be attended by a peculiar sign.* "Behold, he cometh *with clouds.*" We shall have no need to question whether it is the Son of man who has come, or whether he is indeed come. This is to be no secret matter: his coming will be as manifest as yonder clouds. In the wilderness the presence of Jehovah was known by a visible pillar of cloud by day, and an equally visible pillar of fire by night. That pillar of cloud was the sure token that the Lord was in his holy place, dwelling between the cherubim. Such is the token of the coming of the Lord Christ.

> *Every eye the cloud shall scan,*
> *Ensign of the Son of man.*

So it is written, "And then shall appear the sign of the Son of man in heaven: and then shall all the tribes of the earth mourn, and they shall see the Son of man coming in the clouds of heaven with power and great glory." I cannot quote at this time all those many passages of Scripture in which it is indicated that our Lord will come either sitting upon a cloud, or "with the clouds," or "with the clouds of heaven"; but such expressions are abundant. Is it not to show that his coming will be majestic? He makes the clouds his chariots. He comes with hosts of attendants, and these of a nobler sort than earthly monarchs can summon to do them homage. With clouds of angels, cherubim and seraphim, and all the armies of heaven he comes. With all the forces of nature, thundercloud and blackness of tempest, the Lord of all makes his triumphant entrance to judge the world. The clouds are the dust of his feet in that dread day of battle when he shall ease him of his adversaries, shaking them out of the earth with his thunder, and consuming them with the devouring flame of his lightning. All heaven shall gather with its utmost pomp to the great appearing of the Lord, and all the terrible grandeur of nature shall then be seen at its full. Not as the Man of sorrows, despised and rejected of men, shall Jesus come, but as Jehovah came upon Sinai in the midst of thick clouds and a terrible darkness, so shall he come, whose coming shall be the final judgment.

The clouds are meant to set forth the *might*, as well as the majesty, of his coming. "Ascribe ye strength unto God: his excellency is over Israel, and his strength is in the clouds." This was the royal token given by Daniel the prophet in his seventh chapter, at the thirteenth verse, "I saw in the night visions, and, behold, one like the Son of man came with the clouds of heaven." Not less than divine is the glory of the Son of God, who once had not where to lay his head. The sublimest objects in nature shall most fitly minister to the manifest glory of the returning King of men. "Behold, he cometh"; not with the swaddling bands of his infancy, the weariness of his manhood, the shame of his death, but with all the glorious tapestry of heaven's high chambers. The hanging of the divine throne room shall aid his state.

The clouds, also, denote *the terror of his coming to the ungodly*. His saints shall be caught up together with him in the clouds, to meet the Lord in the air; but to those that shall remain on earth the clouds shall turn their blackness and horror of darkness. Then shall the impenitent behold this dread vision— the Son of man coming in the clouds of heaven. The clouds shall fill them with dread, and the dread shall be abundantly justified, for those clouds are big with vengeance, and shall burst in judgment on their heads. His great white throne, though it be bright and lustrous with hope to his people, will with its very brightness and whiteness of immaculate justice strike dead the hopes of all those who trusted that they might live in sin and yet go unpunished. "Behold, he cometh. He cometh with clouds."

I am in happy circumstances tonight, because my subject requires no effort of imagination from me. To indulge fancy on such a theme would be a wretched profanation of so sublime a subject, which in its own simplicity should come home to all hearts. Think clearly for a moment, till the meaning becomes real to you. Jesus Christ is coming, coming in unwonted splendor. When he comes he will be enthroned far above the attacks of his enemies, the persecutions of the godless, and the sneers of skeptics. He is coming in the clouds of heaven, and we shall be among the witnesses of his appearing. Let us dwell upon this truth.

**2. Our second observation is this: *our Lord's coming will be seen of all*.**

"Behold, he cometh with clouds, *and every eye shall see him, and they also which pierced him.*"

I gather from this expression, first, that *it will be a literal appearing, and an actual sight*. If the second advent was to be a spiritual manifestation, to be perceived by the minds of men, the phraseology would be, "Every mind shall perceive him." But it is not so: we read, "Every eye shall see him." Now, the mind can behold the spiritual, but the eye can only see that which is distinctly material and visible. The Lord Jesus Christ will not come spiritually, for in that sense he is always here, but he will come really and substantially, for every eye shall see him, even those unspiritual eyes which gazed on him with hate, and pierced him. Go not away and dream, and say to yourself, "Oh, there is some spiritual meaning about all this." Do not destroy the teaching of the Holy Ghost by the idea that there will be a spiritual manifestation of the Christ of God, but that a literal appearing is out of the question. That would be altering the record. The Lord Jesus shall come to earth a second time as literally as he has come a first time. The same Christ who ate a piece of a broiled fish and of a honeycomb after he had risen from the dead; the same who said, "Handle me, and see; for a spirit hath not flesh and bones, as ye see me have"—this same Jesus, with a material body, is to come in the clouds of heaven. In the same manner as he went up he shall come down. He shall be literally seen. The words cannot be honestly read in any other way.

"Every eye shall see him." Yes, I do literally expect to see my Lord Jesus with these eyes of mine, even as that saint expected who long ago fell asleep, believing that though the worms devoured his body, yet in his flesh he should see God, whom his eyes should see for himself, and not another. There will be a real resurrection of the body, though the moderns doubt it: such a resurrection that we shall see Jesus with our own eyes. We shall not find ourselves in a shadowy, dreamy land of floating fictions, where we may perceive, but cannot see. We shall not be airy nothings, mysterious, vague, impalpable; but we shall literally see our glorious Lord, whose appearing will be no phantom show, or shadow dance. Never day more real than the day of judgment; never sight more true than the Son of man upon the throne of his glory. Will you take this statement home, that you may feel the force of it? We are getting too far away from facts nowadays, and too much into the realm of myths and notions. "Every eye shall see him," in this there shall be no delusion.

Note well that *he is to be seen of all kinds of living men*: every eye shall see him: the king and the peasant, the most learned and the most ignorant. Those that were blind before shall see when he appears. I remember a man born blind who loved our Lord most intensely, and he was inclined to glory in this, that his eyes had been reserved for his Lord. Said he, "The first whom I shall ever see will be the Lord Jesus Christ. The first sight that greets my newly opened eyes will be the Son of man in his glory." There is great comfort in this to all who are now unable to behold the sun. Since "every eye shall see him," you also shall see the King in his beauty. Small pleasure is this to eyes that are full of filthiness and pride: you care not for this sight, and yet you must see it whether you please or do not please. You have thus far shut your eyes to good things, but when Jesus comes you *must* see him. All that dwell upon the face of the earth, if not at the same moment, yet with the same certainty, shall behold the once crucified Lord. They will not be able to hide themselves, nor to hide him from their eyes. They will dread the sight, but it will come upon them, even as the sun shines on the thief who delights in the darkness. They will be obliged to own in dismay that they behold the Son of man: they will be so overwhelmed with the sight that there will be no denying it.

He will be seen of those who have been long since dead. What a sight that will be for Judas and for Pilate and for Caiaphas and for Herod! What a sight it will be for those who, in their lifetime, said that there was no Savior, and no need of one; or that Jesus was a mere man, and that his blood was not a propitiation for sin! Those that scoffed and reviled him have long since died, but they shall all rise again and rise to this heritage among the rest—that they shall see him whom they blasphemed sitting in the clouds of heaven. Prisoners are troubled at the sight of the judge. The trumpet of assize brings no music to the ears of criminals. But you must hear it, O impenitent sinner! Even in your grave you must hear the voice of the Son of God and live and come forth from the tomb, to receive the things done in your body, whether they were good or bad. Death cannot hide you, nor the vault conceal you, nor rottenness and corruption deliver you. You are bound to see in your body the Lord who will judge both you and your fellows.

It is mentioned here that he will especially be seen by those that pierced him. In this is included all the company that nailed him to the tree, with those that took the spear and made the gash in his side; indeed, all that had a hand in his cruel crucifixion. It includes all of these, but it comprehends many more besides. "They also who pierced him" are by no means a few. Who have pierced him? Why those that once professed to love him and have gone back to the world. Those that once ran well, "What did hinder them?" And now they use their tongues to speak against the Christ whom once they professed to love. They also have pierced him whose inconsistent lives have brought dishonor upon the sacred name of Jesus. They also have pierced him, who refused his love, stifled their consciences, and refused his rebukes. Alas, that so many of you should be piercing him now by your base neglect of his salvation! They that went every Sunday to hear of him and that remained hearers only, destroying their own souls rather than yield to his infinite love—these pierced his tender heart. Dear hearers, I wish I could plead effectually with you tonight, so that you would not continue any longer among the number of those that pierced him. If you will look at Jesus now, and mourn for your sin, he will put your sin away; and then you will not be ashamed to see him in that day. Even though you did pierce him, you will be able to sing, "Unto him that loved us, and washed us from our sins in his own blood." But, remember, if you persevere in piercing him, and fighting against him, you will still have to see him in that day, to your terror and despair. He will be seen by you and by me, however ill we may behave. And what horror will that sight cost us!

I felt unfit to preach to you tonight; but last Lord's Day I said that I would preach tonight if I could possibly manage it. It seemed barely possible, but I could not do less than keep my word; and I also longed to be with you, for your sakes; for perhaps there may not remain many more occasions on which I shall be permitted to preach the gospel among you. I am often ill; who knows how soon I shall come to my end? I would use all that remains to me of physical strength and providential opportunity. We never know how soon we may be cut off, and then we are gone forever from the opportunity of benefiting our fellowmen. It were a pity to be taken away with one opportunity of doing good unused. So would I earnestly plead with you under the shadow of this great truth: I would urge you to make ready, since we shall both behold the Lord in the day of his appearing. Yes, I shall stand in that great throng. You also will be there. How will you feel? You are not accustomed, perhaps, to attend a place of worship; but you will be there, and the spot will be very solemn to you. You may absent yourself from the assemblies of the saints, but you will not be able to absent yourself from the gathering of that day. You will be there, one in that great multitude; and you will see Jesus the Lord as truly as if you were the only person before him, and he will look upon you as certainly as if you were the only one that was summoned to his bar.

Will you kindly think of all this as I close this second head? Silently repeat to yourself the words, "Every eye shall see him, and they also that pierced him."

**3. And now I must close with the third head, which is a painful one, but needs to be enlarged upon:** *his coming will cause great sorrow.*

What does the text say about his coming? "All kindreds of the earth shall wail because of him."

"All kindreds of the earth." Then *this sorrow will be very general.* You thought, perhaps, that when Christ came, he would come to a glad world, welcoming him with song and music. You thought that there might be a few ungodly persons who would be destroyed with the breath of his month, but that the bulk of mankind would receive him with delight. See how different—"All kindreds of the earth," that is, all sorts of men that belong to the earth; all earthborn men, men out of all nations and kindreds and tongues shall weep and wail, and gnash their teeth at his coming. O sirs, this is a sad outlook! We have no smooth things to prophesy. What think you of this?

And, next, *this sorrow will be very great.* They shall *"wail."* I cannot put into English the full meaning of that most expressive word. Sound it at length, and it conveys its own meaning. It is as when men wring their hands and burst out into a loud cry; or as when eastern women, in their anguish, rend their garments, and lift up their voices with the most mournful notes. All the kindreds of the earth shall wail: wail as a mother laments over her dead child; wail as a man might wail who found himself hopelessly imprisoned and doomed to die. Such will be the hopeless grief of all the kindreds of the earth at the sight of Christ in the clouds: if they remain impenitent, they shall not be able to be silent; they shall not be able to repress or conceal their anguish, but they shall wail or openly give vent to their horror. What a sound that will be which will go up before high heaven when Jesus sits upon the cloud, and in the fullness of his power summons them to judgment! Then "they shall wail because of him."

Will your voice be heard in that wailing? Will your heart be breaking in that general dismay? How will you escape? If you are one of the kindreds of the earth and remain impenitent, you will wail with the rest of them. Unless you now fly to Christ, and hide yourself in him, and so become one of the kindred of heaven—one of his chosen and blood-washed ones, who shall praise his name for washing them from their sins—unless you do this, there will be wailing at the judgment seat of Christ, and you will be in it.

Then it is quite clear that men will not be universally converted when Christ comes; because, if they were so, they would not wail. Then they would lift up the cry, "Welcome, welcome, Son of God!" The coming of Christ would be as the hymn puts it—

> *Hark, those bursts of acclamation!*
> *Hark, those loud triumphant chords!*
> *Jesus takes the highest station.*
> *Oh, what joy the sight affords!*

These acclamations come from his people. But according to the text the multitude of mankind will weep and wail, and therefore they will not be among his people. Do not, therefore, look for salvation to some coming day, but believe in Jesus now, and find in him your Savior at once. If you joy in him now, you shall much more rejoice in him in that day, but if you will have cause to wail at his coming, it will be well to wail at once.

Note one more truth. It is quite certain that when Jesus comes in those latter days *men will not be expecting great things of him.* You know the talk they have nowadays about "a larger hope." Today they deceive the people with the idle dream of repentance and restoration after death, a fiction unsupported by the least tittle of Scripture. If these kindreds of the earth expected that when Christ would come they would all die out and cease to be, they would rejoice that thereby they escaped the wrath of God. Would not each unbeliever say, "It were a consummation devoutly to be wished"? If they thought that at his coming there would be a universal restoration and a general jail delivery of souls long shut up in prison, would they wail? If Jesus could be supposed to come to proclaim a general restoration, they would not wail, but shout for joy. Ah no! It is because his coming to the impenitent is black with blank despair that they will wail because of him. If his first coming does not give you eternal life, his second coming will not. If you do not hide in his wounds when he comes as your Savior, there will be no hiding place for you when he comes as your Judge. They will weep and wail because, having rejected the Lord Jesus, they have turned their backs on the last possibility of hope.

Why do they wail *because of him*? Will it not be because they will see him in his glory, and they will recollect that they slighted and despised him? They will see him come to judge them, and they will remember that once he stood at their door with mercy in his hands and said, "Open to me," but they would not admit him. They refused his blood: they refused his righteousness: they trifled with his sacred name; and now they must give an account for this wickedness. They put him away in scorn, and now, when he comes, they find that they can trifle with him no longer. The days of child's play and of foolish delay are over; and now they have solemnly to give in their life's account. See, the books are opened! They are covered with dismay as they remember their sins, and know that they are written down by a faithful pen. They must give an account; and unwashed and unforgiven they cannot render that account without knowing that the sentence will be, "Depart, ye cursed." This is why they weep and wail because of him.

O souls, my natural love of ease makes me wish that I could preach pleasant things to you; but they are not in my commission. I need scarce wish, however, to preach a soft gospel, for so many are already doing it to your cost. As I love your immortal souls, I dare not flatter you. As I shall have to answer for it in the last great day, I must tell you the truth.

*Ye sinners seek his face*
*Whose wrath ye cannot bear.*

Seek the mercy of God tonight. I have come here in pain to implore you to be reconciled to God. "Kiss the Son lest he be angry, and ye perish from the way, when his wrath is kindled but a little. Blessed are all they that put their trust in him."

But if you will not have my Lord Jesus, he comes all the same for that. He is on the road now, and when he comes you will wail because of him. Oh, that you would make him your friend, and then meet him with joy! Why will you die? He gives life to all those who trust him. Believe, and live.

God save your souls tonight, and he shall have the glory. Amen.

# Preparation for the Coming of the Lord

Delivered on Lord's Day morning, September 22, 1889, at the Metropolitan Tabernacle, Newington. No. 2105.

> *And now, little children, abide in him; that, when he shall appear, we may have confidence, and not be ashamed before him at his coming.* —1 John 2:28

Our first anxious desire is that our hearers would come to Christ. We lay ourselves out to lift him up, as Moses lifted up the serpent in the wilderness, and to bid men look to him and live. There is no salvation except by faith in the Lord Jesus Christ. He said, "Look unto me, and be ye saved, all the ends of the earth: for I am God, and there is none else."

When men have looked to Jesus, our next anxiety is that they may be in Christ, the city of refuge. We long to speak of them as "men in Christ Jesus." My beloved hearers, you must be in living, loving, lasting union with the Son of God, or else you are not in a state of salvation. That which begins with coming to Christ, as the engrafted branch is bound to the vine, continues in your growing into him and receiving of his life. You must be in Christ as the stone is in the building, as the member is in the body.

When we have good hope that our hearers have come to Christ, and are "in Christ," a further anxiety springs up in our hearts that they may "abide" in Christ. Our longing is that, despite temptations to go away from him, they may always remain at his feet; that, notwithstanding the evil of their nature, they may never betray their Master, but may faithfully hold to him. We would have them mindful of that precept, "As ye have received Christ Jesus the Lord, so walk ye in him." Oh, that they may be rooted in him, and built up in him, and may always be in union with him! Then shall we present them to our Lord in the day of his appearing with exceeding great joy.

To this third anxiety of the minister of Christ I would give my mind this morning. John says, "Little children, abide in him." How sweetly those words must have flowed from the lips and the pen of such a venerable saint! I think he is in this the echo of the Lord Jesus; for in the fifteenth chapter of the Gospel of John, the Lord Jesus said, "Abide in me, and I in you. As the branch cannot bear fruit of itself, except it abide in the vine, no more can you, except you abide in me. If you abide in me, and my words abide in you, you shall ask what you will, and it shall be done unto you." That word, "abide," was a very favorite one with the Lord Jesus, and it became equally dear to that disciple whom Jesus loved. In our Authorized Version, the translators have interpreted it sometimes "remain," and sometimes "continue"; but it is not very wise of them to have so changed the rendering. It is one of the virtues of the Revised Version that it generally translates the same Greek word by the same English word. This may not be absolutely requisite, for a little variety may be tolerated; but it is eminently instructive, since it allows us to see in our own mother tongue where the Holy Spirit used the same word; and if the translation be correct in one case, we may naturally conclude it will not be incorrect in another. "Abide" is one of John's special words.

May the Lord help us to consider these blessed words! Better still, may he write them on our hearts, and may we fulfill their teaching!

First, notice *to what he urges them*—"abide in him"; second, *under what character he addresses them*—"little children"; and third, *by what motive he exhorts them*—"that, when he shall appear, we may have confidence, and not be ashamed before him at his coming."

## 1. First, then, observe *to what he urges them*: "abide in him."

By this he meant one thing; but that thing is so comprehensive that we may better understand it by viewing it from many sides.

He meant fidelity to the truth taught by our Lord. We are sure he meant this, because, a little previously, in the twenty-fourth verse, he had said, "If that which ye have heard from the beginning shall remain in you, ye also shall continue in the Son, and in the Father." Beloved, you have believed in the Lord Jesus Christ unto the salvation of your souls. You have trusted in him as the Son of God, the appointed Mediator, and the effectual sacrifice for your sin. Your hope has come from a belief in Christ as God has borne witness to him. Abide in the truth which you received from the beginning; for in your earliest days it worked salvation in you. The foundation of your faith is not a changeable doctrine: you rest on a sure word of testimony. Truth is, in its very nature, fixed and unalterable. You know more about it than you did; but the thing itself is still the same, and must be the same. Take care that you abide in it. You will find it difficult to do so, for there is an element of changeableness about yourself: this you must overcome by grace. You will find many elements of seduction in the outside world. There are men whose business it is to shake the faith of others, and thereby to gain a repute for cleverness and depth of thought. Some seem to think it an ambition worthy of a Christian to be always questioning, or, as the apostle puts it, to be "ever learning, and never able to come to the knowledge of the truth." To throw doubt into minds which, by a gracious certainty, have been made blessed, is their chosen life-work. Therefore, you will be often led to try your foundation, and at times you will tremble as you cling to it. Hearken, then, to this word from the mouth of your Lord: "abide in him." Keep you where you were as to the truth which you believe. That which has justified you, will sanctify you. That which has, in a measure, sanctified you, will yet perfect you. Make no change as to the eternal verities upon which you ground your hope. As a stone, you are built on the foundation; abide there. As a branch, you have been grafted into the stem; abide there. As a member, you are in the body; abide there; it is all over with you if you do not. Abide in that holy mold of doctrine into which you were at first delivered. Let no man deceive you with vain words, though there are many abroad in these days who "would deceive, if it were possible, the very elect." Abide in Jesus, by letting his words abide in you. Believe what you have found to be the means of your quickening. Believe it with a greater intensity and a greater practicalness; but "cast not away your confidence, which hath great recompense of reward."

Next, he means "abide in him" *as to the uniformity of your trust.* When you first enjoyed a hope, you rested upon Christ alone. I think I heard the first infant prattle of your faith when it said,

> *I'm a poor sinner and nothing at all,*
> *But Jesus Christ is my all in all.*

At the first, you had no experience upon which you could rely, you had no inward graces upon which you could depend: you rested wholly upon Christ and his finished work. You rested in no degree upon the works of the law, nor upon your own feelings, nor upon your own knowledge, nor upon your own resolves. Christ was all. Do you not remember how you used to tell others that the gospel precept was "only believe"? You cried to them, "Trust in Jesus; get out of yourselves; find all your wants provided for in him." Now, beloved, you have experience; thank God for it. Now you have the graces of the Spirit; thank God for them. Now you know the things of God by the teaching of the Holy Spirit; be grateful for that knowledge. But do not now fly in the face of your Savior by putting your experience, or your graces, or your knowledge, where he and he alone must be. Depend today as simply as you depended then. If you have some idea that you are hastening toward perfection, take care that you do not indulge a vain conceit of yourself; but even if it be true, still mix not your perfection with his perfection, nor your advance in grace with the foundation which he has laid for you in his blood and righteousness. "Abide in him." He is that good ship into which you have entered that he may bear you safe to the desired haven. Abide in the vessel: neither venture to walk on the water, like Peter, nor think to swim by your own strength; but "abide in him," and you shall weather every storm. Only as you keep to your first simple confidence in the perfect work of the Lord Jesus can you have peace and salvation; as it is written, "Thou wilt keep him in perfect peace, whose mind is stayed on thee; because he trusteth in thee."

Moreover, abide in the Lord Jesus Christ in making him the constant object of your life. As you live by Christ, so live for Christ. Ever since you trusted in Christ as dying for you, you have felt that if he died for you, then you died in him, that henceforth your life might be consecrated to him. You are not your own, but you are Christ's, and Christ's only. The first object of your being is to honor and serve him who loved you and gave himself for you. You have not followed after wealth or honor or self-pleasing, but you have followed Jesus: take heed that you "abide in him" by continuing to serve him. "Love not the world, neither the things that are in the world. If any man love the world, the love of the Father is not in him. For all that is in the world, the lust of the flesh, and the lust of the eyes, and the pride of life, is not of the Father, but is of the world. And the world passes away, and the lust thereof: but he that does the will of God abides forever." You may wisely continue where you are, for you have chosen the right pursuit, and you have entered upon the right road. That crown which glitters in your eye at the end of the race is worthy of all your running. You could not have a nobler motive power than the constraining love of Christ. To live for Christ is the highest style of living: continue in it more and more. If the Lord changes your circumstances, still live for Christ. If you go up, take Christ up with you: if you go down, Christ will go down with you. If you are in health, live for Christ earnestly; if you are bound to a sick bed, live for Christ patiently. Go about your business and sing for Jesus; or if he bids you stay at home, and cough away your life, then sicken for Jesus; but let everything be for him. For you, "excelsior" means higher consecration, more heavenly living.

Surely, we should also understand by "abide in him," that we are to persevere in our obedience to our Lord. The next verse is, "If ye know that he is righteous, ye know that everyone that doeth righteousness is born of him." What your Lord bids you, continue to do. Call no man "master," but in all things submit your thoughts, your words, and your acts to the rule of the Lord Jesus. Obey him by whose obedience you are justified. Be precise and prompt in your execution of his commands. If others reckon you morbidly conscientious, heed not their opinion, but "abide in him." The rule of the master is always binding on all his disciples, and they depart from him in heart when they err from his rule. Reverence for the precept is as much included in our homage of Christ as credence of the doctrine. If you have been upright in your dealings, be upright; be accurate to the penny in every payment. If you have been loving and generous, continue loving and generous; for your Lord's law is love. If you have closely imitated the Lord Jesus, go on to copy him still more minutely. Seek no new model; pray the Holy Spirit to work you to the selfsame thing. To you, as a soldier, your Captain's word is law:

> *Yours is not to reason why,*
> *Yours is but to dare and die.*

"Abide in him." I know you might be rich by doing that un-Christly act; scorn to win wealth in such a way. I know you may involve yourself in persecution if you follow your Lord closely. Accept such persecution gladly, and rejoice in it, for his name's sake. I know that a great many would say that for charity's sake you had better make compromises, and keep in union with evil doctrine and worldly practice; but you know better. Be it yours to follow the Lamb whithersoever he goes; for this is what his beloved apostle means when he says, "Abide in him."

But I have not completed the full description yet; I fear I am not able to do so, by reason of my shallow knowledge and forgetfulness. *Continue in spiritual union with your Lord.* All the life you have is life derived from him; seek no other. You are not a Christian except as Jesus is the Christ of God to you; you are not alive unto God, except as you are one with the risen Lord. You are not saved, except as he is your Savior; nor righteous, save as he is your Righteousness. You have not a single pulse of heavenly desire, nor a breath of divine life in you, but what was first given you from him, and is daily given to you by him. Abide in this vital union. Do not try to lead an independent life. "Abide in him," in complete dependence from day to day upon the life which is treasured up in him on your behalf.

Let your life "abide in him" in the sense of being directed by him. The head directs all the members. The order which lifts my hand, or spreads my palm, or closes my fist, or lowers my arm, comes from the brain, which is the headquarters of the soul. Abide in your Lord by implicitly owning his headship. Let every regulation of your life come from him who is the head, and let it be obeyed as naturally as the desires of the mind coming from the brain are obeyed by every part of the body. There is no war between the hand and the foot, for they abide in the head, and so are ruled without force, and guided without violence. If the leg were to set up an independent authority over itself, instead of obeying the head, what strange walking we should see! Have you never met with afflicted people in whom the nerves have lost vigor, and the muscles seem to jerk at random, and throw out a leg or an arm without reason? Such movements are painful to see, and we know that such a man is diseased. Do not desire to be without law to Christ. Let that mind be in you which was also in Christ Jesus: in that respect "abide in him."

"Abide in him" as the element of your life. Let him encompass you as the air surrounds you on all sides. As a fish, whether it be the tiniest sprat or the hugest whale, abides in the sea, so do you abide in Christ. The fish does not seek the sky or the shore, it could not live out of the element of water; and even so, I beseech you, do not seek to live in the world and in its sins; for as a Christian you cannot live there: Christ is your life. There is room enough for you in the Lord Jesus Christ, for he is the infinite God. Go not out of him for anything. Seek not pleasure outside of Christ, nor treasure outside of Christ; for such pleasure or treasure would be ruinous. Have neither want, nor will, nor wish, beyond your Lord. Let him draw a line around you, and do you abide within that circle.

"Abide in him" in the sense of being at home in him. What a world of meaning I intend by that word "being at home in Christ"! and yet this is the sense of the word "abide in him." I was speaking yesterday to a friend who had bought a pleasant house, with a large garden; and he said to me, "I now feel as if I had a home. I have lived in London for years, and I have changed from one house to another with as little regret as a man feels in changing an omnibus; but I have always longed for the home feeling which hung about my father's house in the country. Why, there we loved the cozy rooms, and the lookouts from the little windows, and the corner cupboards in the kitchen. As for the garden and the field, they yielded us constant delight, for there was that bush in the garden where the robin had built, and the tree with the blackbird's nest. We knew where the pike lay in the pool, and where the tortoise had buried itself for the winter, and where the first primroses would be found in the spring. There is a vast difference between a house and a home." That is what John means with regard to Christ: we are not merely to call on him, but to abide in him. Do not go to Jesus one day and to the world another day: do not be a lodger with him, but abide in him. My friend spoke of changing from one omnibus to another, and I fear that some change from Christ to the world when the day changes from Sunday to Monday; but it should not be so. Say with Moses, "Lord, thou hast been our dwelling place in all generations." Your cross is the rooftree of the family of love; within the thorn hedge of your suffering love our whole estate is shut in; your name is named on our abiding place. We are not to you as tenants with a lease, but we have a freehold in you. We can truly say and sing—

> *Here would I make a settled rest*
> *While others go and come:*
> *No more a stranger or a guest,*
> *But like a child at home.*

Lord Jesus, I am at home nowhere but in you; but in you I abide. Wherever else I lodge, I have in due time to shift my quarters. Whatever else I have, I lose it, or leave it; but you are the same, and you change not. What a comfort to have our Lord himself to be our chosen dwelling place in time and in eternity!

Now I think I have come nearer to the full sense of my text. "Abide in him" means, hold fast to him, live in him, let all your noblest powers be drawn forth in connection with him, as a man at home is all there. Feel at ease in fellowship with him. Say, "Return unto thy rest, O my soul; for the Lord hath dealt bountifully with thee."

Why does the apostle urge us to abide in Christ? Is there any likelihood of our going away? Yes; for in this very chapter he mentions apostates, who from disciples had degenerated into antichrists, of whom he says, "They went out from us, but they were not of us; for if they had been of us they would, no doubt, have continued with us." "Abide in him," then, and do not turn aside unto crooked ways, as many professors have done. The Savior once said to his apostles, "Will ye also go away?," and they answered him with that other question, "Lord, to whom shall we go?" I hope your heart is so conscious that he has the words of eternal life that you could not dream of going elsewhere.

"But surely it is implied in these warnings that saints do leave their Lord and perish?" I answer, "No." Carefully observe the provision which is made against that fatality—provision to enable us to carry out the precept of the text. Will you open your Testaments, and just look at the verse which immediately precedes my text? What do you see? "Ye shall abide in him. And now, little children, abide in him." There is a promise made to those who are in Christ that they shall "abide in him"; but that promise does not render the precept unnecessary; for the Lord deals with us as with reasonable beings, not as with sticks and stones; and he secures the fulfillment of his own promise that we shall abide in him, by impressing upon our hearts his sacred precept, whereby he bids us "abide in him." The force he uses to effect his purpose is instruction, heart winning, and persuading. We abide in him, not by a physical law, as a mass of iron abides on the earth; but by a mental and spiritual law, by which the greatness of divine love and goodness holds us fast to the Lord Jesus. You have the guarantee that you shall abide in Christ in the covenant engagement, "I will put my fear in their hearts, that they shall not depart from me." What a blessed promise that is! You are to take care that you abide in Christ as much as if all depended upon yourself; and yet you can look to the promise of the covenant, and see that the real reason for your abiding in Christ lies in the operation of his unchanging love and grace.

Moreover, brethren, if you are in Christ Jesus, you have the Holy Ghost given you to enable you to abide in him. Read the twenty-seventh verse: "But the anointing which ye have received of him abideth in you, and ye need not that any man teach you: but as the same anointing teacheth you of all things, and is truth, and is no lie, and even as it hath taught you, ye shall abide in him."

The Holy Ghost brings the truth home to your heart with savor and unction, endearing it to your inmost soul. The truth has so saturated you through the anointing, that you cannot give it up. Has not your Lord said, "The water that I shall give him shall be in him a well of water springing up unto everlasting life"? Thus, you see that what is commanded in one Scripture is promised and provided for in another. To his people, God's commandings are enablings. As he bids you abide in him, so by that very bidding he causes you to abide in him to his praise and glory.

## 2. Second, notice *under what character John addresses these believers.*

He says, "And now, *little children.*" This indicates *the apostle's love to them.* John lived to a great age; and the tradition is, that they used to carry him into the assembly, and, when he could do nothing else, he would lift his hand, and simply say, "Little children, love one another." Here, to show his tender concern for those to whom he wrote, he called them "little children." He could not wish them a greater blessing out of the depth of his heart's affection, than that they should faithfully abide in Christ.

Next, by this he suggests their near and dear relation to their Father in heaven. You are the children of God; but as yet you are little ones, therefore do not leave your Father's house, nor run away from your elder brother's love. Because you are little children, you are not of traveling years, therefore stay at home and abide in your Lord.

Does he not hint at their feebleness? Even if you were grown and strong, you would not be wise to gather all together and wander away into the far country; but as you are so young, so dependent, so feeble, it is essential that you abide in him. Shall a babe forsake its mother? What can you do apart from God? Is he not your life, your all?

Does not the apostle also gently hint at *their fickleness*? You are very changeable, like little babes. You are apt to be hot and cold in half an hour. You are this and that, and fifty other things, in the course of one revolving moon. But, little children as you are, be faithful to one point—abide in your Savior. Change not toward your Redeemer. Stretch out your hands and clasp him and cry,

> *My Jesus, I love thee, I knew thou art mine,*
> *For thee all the follies of sin I resign.*

Surrender yourself to him by an everlasting covenant never to be canceled. Be his forever and ever.

Did not this remind them of their daily dependence upon the Lord's care, as little children depend on their parents? Why, beloved, the Lord has to nurse you. He feeds you with the unadulterated milk of the Word; he comforts you as a mother does her child; he carries you in his bosom, he bears you all your days. Your new life is as yet weak and struggling; do not carry it into the cold atmosphere of distance from Jesus. Little children, since you derive all from Jesus, abide in him. To go elsewhere will be to wander into a howling wilderness. The world is empty; only Christ has fullness. Away from Jesus you will be as a child deserted by its mother, left to pine, and starve, and die; or as a little lamb on the hillside without a shepherd, tracked by the wolf, whose teeth will soon extract its heart's blood. Abide, O child, with your mother! Abide, O lamb, with your shepherd!

We may all come under John's description at this time. The beloved John speaks unto us as unto little children, for we are none of us much more. We are not such wonderfully knowing people as certain of our neighbors; we are not such learned scientists and acute critics as they are; neither have we their marvelous moral consciousness, which is superior to inspiration itself; therefore we are bound by our very feebleness to venture less than they do. Let the men of the world choose what paths they will, we feel bound to abide in Christ because we know no other place of safety. They may push off into the sea of speculation; our smaller boats must hug the shore of certainty. To us, however, it is no small comfort that the Lord has revealed to babes the things which are hidden from the wise and prudent. Those who become as little children enter into the kingdom of heaven.

Cling to the Lord Jesus in your feebleness, in your fickleness, in your nothingness; and abidingly take him to be everything to you. "The coneys are but a feeble folk, yet make they their houses in the rocks"; be you like them. Abide in the rifts of the Rock of ages, and let nothing tempt you to quit your stronghold. You are no lion, able to fight your foes, and deliver yourself by main strength; you are only a little coney, and you will be wise to hide rather than fight. "Little children, abide in him."

3. I now come to my last point, which is most important, for it finds steam wherewith to drive the engine. Third, we shall consider *by what motive John exhorts us to this pleasant and necessary duty of abiding in Christ.*

Kindly look at the text, for there is in it a little word to be noticed. The apostle exhorts us *by a motive in which he takes his share.* Let me read it: "Now, little children, abide in him; that, when he shall appear, you may have confidence." No, no. Look at that little word: it runs thus, "that *we* may have confidence." The beloved John needed to have confidence at the appearing of the Lord, and confidence fetched from the same source as that to which he directed his little children. They must abide in Christ, that they might have confidence, and the dearest of the apostles must practice the same abiding. How wisely, and yet how sweetly, he puts himself upon our level in this matter!

Notice, further, that the motive is one *drawn from Jesus.* John does not drive believers with the lash of the law, but he draws them with the cords of love. I never like to see God's children whipped with rods gathered from the thorny sides of Sinai. We have not come to Mount Sinai, but to Mount Zion. When a man tries to pommel me to my duty by the law, I kick at the goad like a bullock unaccustomed to the yoke; and rightly so, "For you are not under the law, but under grace." The motive which sways a freeborn heir of heaven is fetched from grace, and not from law; from Jesus, and not from Moses. Christ is our example, and our motive also, blessed be his name!

*The motive is drawn from our Lord's expected advent.* Notice how John puts it. He uses two words for the same thing: "when he shall appear" and "at his coming." The second advent may be viewed in two lights. First, as the appearing of one who is here already, but is hidden; and next, as the coming of one who is absent. In the first sense, we know that our Lord Jesus Christ abides in his church; according to his word, "Lo, I am with you always, even unto the end of the world." Yet, though spiritually present, he is unseen. Our Lord will, on a sudden, be "manifested," as the Revised Version has it. The spiritual and secret presence of Christ will become a visible and manifest presence in the day of his appearing.

The apostle also uses the term "at his coming" or "his presence." This is the same thing from another point of view. In a certain evident sense our Lord is absent: "He is not here, for he is risen." He has gone his way unto the Father. In that respect he will come a second time, "without a sin offering, unto salvation." He who has gone from us will so come in like manner as he was seen to go up into heaven. There is thus a difference of aspect between the second advent when it is described as "his appearing" and "his coming." John pleads the glorious manifestation of our Lord under both of these views as a reason for abiding in him.

As to our Lord's "appearing," he would have us abide in Christ, that we may have confidence when he appears. Confidence at his appearing is the high reward of constant abiding in Christ. The apostle keeps most prominent "the appearing" as an argument. A thousand things are to happen at our Lord's appearing; but John does not mention one of them. He does not hold it up as a thing to be desired that we may have confidence amid the wreck of matter and the crash of worlds, when the stars shall fall like autumn leaves, when the sun shall be turned into darkness, and the moon into blood; when the graves shall be opened, and the dead shall rise, or when the heavens, being on fire, shall be dissolved, and the elements shall melt with fervent heat, the earth also, and the works that are therein, shall be burned up. Those will be direful times, days of terror and dismay; but it is not of these that he speaks particularly; for he regards all these events as swallowed up in the one great fact of the glorious appearing of our Lord and Savior Jesus Christ.

His desire is that we may have confidence if he appear on a sudden. What does he mean by having confidence when he shall appear? Why, this: that if you abide in him when you do not see him, you will be very bold should he suddenly reveal himself. Before he appears, you have dwelt in him, and he has dwelt in you; what fear could his appearing cause you? Faith has so realized him, that if suddenly he were to appear to the senses, it would be no surprise to you; and, assuredly, it would cause you joy rather than dismay. You would feel that you at last enjoyed what you had long expected, and saw somewhat more closely a friend with whom you had long been familiar. I trust, beloved, that some of us live in such a style that if, on a sudden, our Lord were to appear, it would cause no alarm to us. We have believed him to be present, though unseen, and it will not affect our conduct when he steps from behind the curtain and stands in the open light. O Lord Jesus, if you were now to stand in our midst, we should remember that we had your presence before, and lived in it, and now we should only be the more assured of that which we before knew by faith. We shall behold our Lord with confidence, freedom, assurance, and delight, feeling perfectly at home with him. The believer who abides in his Lord would be but little startled by his sudden appearing; he is serving his Lord now, and he would go on serving him; he loves him now, and he would go on loving him, only as he would have a clearer view of him, he would feel a more intense consecration to him.

The word translated "confidence" means freedom of speech. If our divine Lord were to appear in a moment, we should not lose our tongue through fear, but should welcome him with glad acclaim. To desert our Lord would rob us of that ease of mind which is shown by free speech; but to cleave to him will secure us confidence. We now speak to him in secret, and he speaks again to us; we shall not cease to speak in tones of reverent love when he appears. I have preached concerning my Lord, while he is not seen, those truths which I shall not blush to own before his face. If my Lord and Master were, at this instant, to appear in his glory in this tabernacle, I dare with confidence hand in to him the volumes of my sermons, in proof that I have not departed from his truth, but have heartily continued in him. I ought to improve in many things, but I could not improve upon the gospel which I have preached among you. I am prepared to live by it, to die by it, or to meet my Lord upon it if he should this day appear. O my hearers, if you are in Christ, see to it that you so abide in him that, should he suddenly appear, you would behold him with confidence. If we abide in him, if he were to unveil his majestic face, we might be overcome with rapture, but our confidence in him would grow stronger, our freedom with him would be even more enlarged, and our joy in him would be made perfect. Has he not prayed for us that we may be with him, and behold his glory; and can we be afraid of the answer to his loving prayer? If you abide in Christ, the manifestation of Christ will be your manifestation, and that will be a matter of delight, and not of fear.

Beloved, if you do not abide in him, you will have no confidence. If I were to compromise the truth, and then my Lord were to appear, could I meet him with confidence? If, to preserve my reputation, or be thought liberal minded, I played fast and loose with the gospel, how could I see my Lord's face with confidence? If any of you have failed to serve your Master; if you have preferred gain to godliness, and pleasure to holiness; if he were suddenly to shine forth in his glory, what confidence could you have in meeting him? A good man was asked, one day, "If the Lord were now to appear, how would you feel?" He replied. "My brother, I should not be afraid; but I think I should be ashamed." He meant that he was not afraid of condemnation, but he blushed to think how little he had served his Lord. In this case it was genuine humility. I pray you, get not only beyond being afraid, but may the Lord make you so to abide in him that you would not even be ashamed at his appearing!

The other point is, that you should "not be ashamed before him at his coming." That means, that having regarded him as being absent, you have not so lived that, if he should suddenly be present in person, you would be ashamed of your past life. What must it be to be driven with shame away from his presence into everlasting contempt? The text may have such a meaning. What have you been doing while he has been absent? This is a question for a servant to answer at his Lord's arrival. You are left in his house to take care of it while he is in the far-off country; and if you have been beating his servants, and eating and drinking with the drunken, you will be greatly ashamed when he returns. His coming will be in itself a judgment. "Who may abide the day of his coming? And who shall stand when he appears?" Blessed is that man who, with all his faults, has been so sanctified by grace that he will not be ashamed at his Lord's coming. Who is that man? It is the man who has learned to abide in Christ. What is the way to prepare for Christ's coming? By the study of the prophecies? Yes, if you are sufficiently instructed to be able to understand them. "To be prepared for the Lord's coming," some enthusiasts might say, "had I not better spend a month in retirement, and get out of this wicked world?" You may, if you like; and especially you will do so if you are lazy. But the one scriptural prescription for preparing for his coming is this: "abide in him." If you abide in the faith of him, holding his truth, following his example, and making him your dwelling place, your Lord may come at any hour, and you will welcome him. The cloud, the great white throne, the blast of trumpets, the angelic attendants of the last assize, the trembling of creation, and the rolling up of the universe as a worn-out vesture, will have no alarms for you; for you will not be ashamed at his coming.

The date of that coming is concealed. When he shall come, no man can tell. Watch for him, and be always ready, that you may not be ashamed at his advent. Should a Christian man go into worldly assemblies and amusements? Would he not be ashamed should his Lord come and find him among the enemies of the cross? I dare not go where I should be ashamed to be found should my Lord come on a sudden. Should a Christian man ever be in a passion? Suppose his Lord should there and then come; would he not be ashamed at his coming? One here says of an offender, "I will never forgive her; she shall never darken my doors again." Would you not be ashamed if the Lord Jesus came, and found you unforgiving? Oh, that we may abide in him, and never be in such a state that his coming would be unwelcome to us! Beloved, so live from day to day in duty and in devotion, that your Lord's coming would be timely. Go about your daily business and abide in him, and then his coming will be a glorious delight to you. I called to see one of our friends, and she was whitening the front steps of the house. She apologized very much, and said that she felt ashamed of being caught in such a position; but I assured her that I should like my Lord to come and find me, just as I found her, doing my daily work with all my heart. We are never in better trim for seeing our Master than when we are faithfully doing his work. There is no need for a pious smartening up; he that abides in Christ always wears garments of glory and beauty; he may go in with his Lord into the wedding whenever the midnight cry is heard. Abide in him, and then none can make you ashamed. Who shall lay anything to your charge?

He will come—behold, he is coming even now. Hear you not the sounding of his chariot wheels? He may arrive before yon sun goes down. "In such an hour as ye think not, the Son of man cometh." When the world is eating and drinking, marrying and giving in marriage, he will bring destruction upon the ungodly. Be you so engaged, day by day, that you will not be taken at unawares. What will it be to be caught up together with the saints in the clouds, to meet the Lord in the air? What will it be to see him come in the glory of the Father, and all his holy angels with him? What will it be to see him reign upon the earth, with his ancients gloriously? Can you imagine the millennial splendor, the age of gold, the halcyon days of peace? As for the judgment of the world, know you not that the saints shall judge angels? They shall appear as assessors with Christ, and the Lord shall bruise Satan under their feet. Glory awaits us, and nothing but glory, if we abide in Christ. Therefore, keep your garments unspotted, your loins girded, your lamps trimmed, and your lights burning, and you yourselves as men that look for your Lord, that, when he comes, you may have confidence, and not shame. May the Holy Spirit, without whom this cannot be, be freely given to us this day, that we may abide in the Lord! And you who have never trusted in Christ for salvation, may you come to him, and then "abide in him" from this good hour! To his name be glory! Amen.

# Watching for Christ's Coming

~⁕~

Intended for reading on Lord's Day, April 2, 1893; delivered on Lord's Day evening, April 7, 1889, at the Metropolitan Tabernacle, Newington. No. 2302.

> *Blessed are those servants, whom the lord when he cometh shall find watching: verily I say unto you, that he shall gird himself, and make them to sit down to meat, and will come forth and serve them. And if he shall come in the second watch, or come in the third watch, and find them so, blessed are those servants.* —LUKE 12:37–38

I am about to speak of the second coming of Christ; and I felt thankful that my dear brother's prayer, although we had not been in consultation with one another upon the matter, was in every way so suitable to the subject upon which I am to speak. He led us in prayer to think of our coming Lord; so that I trust you are on the margin of the subject now, and that you will not have to make any very great exertion of mind to plunge into midstream, and be carried away with the full current of thought concerning the second advent of the Savior. It is a very appropriate topic when we come to the Lord's table; for, as that prayer reminded us, the Lord's Supper looks backward and is a memorial of his agony; but it looks forward and is an anticipation of his glory. Paul wrote to the church at Corinth, "For as often as ye eat this bread, and drink this cup, ye do show the Lord's death till he come." By looking forward, in a right state of heart, to that second coming of Christ which is the joy of his church, you will be also in a right state of heart for coming to the communion table. May the Holy Ghost make it to be so!

The posture at the communion table, as you know, according to our Lord's example, was not that of kneeling, but that of reclining. The easiest position which you can assume is the most fitting for the Lord's Supper; and yet remember that the supper was no sooner finished than "they sang a hymn," and when that hymn was concluded, they went out into the Mount of Olives to the agonies of Gethsemane. It often seems to me as if now, after finding rest at the table by feeding upon Christ, whose real presence we have, not after a carnal sort, but after a spiritual sort, after that, we sing a hymn, as if we would go out to meet our Lord in his second coming, not going to the Mount of Olives to see him in a bloody sweat, but to hear that word of the angel, "This same Jesus, which is taken up from you into heaven, shall so come in like manner as ye have seen him go into heaven." I do not think we ought to feel at all surprised if we were to go out from the table of fellowship tonight, and meet our Lord at once; no, we should be always waiting for his appearing, ever expecting him, not knowing at what hour the Master of the house shall come. The world does not expect him; it goes on with its eating and drinking, its marrying and giving in marriage; but his own family should expect him. When he will return from the wedding, I trust that he will not find the door shut against him, but that we shall be ready to open to our Lord immediately he knocks. That is the object of the few words that I shall have to say tonight, to stir you up, and my own heart also, to be ever watching for Christ's second coming.

**1. First,** *the Lord will come.* **He that has come once is to come again; he will come a second time. The Lord will come.**

He will come again, for *he has promised to return.* We have his own word for it. That is our first reason for expecting him. Among the last of the words which he spoke to his servant John are these, "Surely I come quickly." You may read it, "I am coming quickly. I am even now upon the road. I am traveling as fast as wisdom allows. I am always coming and coming quickly." Our Lord has promised to come, and to come in person. Some try to explain the second coming of Christ as though it meant the believer dying. You may, if you like, consider that Christ comes to his saints in death. In a certain sense, he does; but that sense will never bear out the full meaning of the teaching of the second advent with which the Scripture is full. No, "the Lord himself shall descend from heaven with a shout, with the voice of the archangel, and with the trump of God." He who went up to heaven will come down from heaven, and stand in the latter day upon the earth. Every redeemed soul can say with Job, "Though after my skin worms destroy this body, yet in my flesh shall I see God: whom I shall see for myself, and mine eyes shall behold, and not another." Christ will as certainly be here again in glory as he once was here in shame, for he has promised to return.

Moreover, *the great scheme of redemption requires Christ's return.* It is a part of that scheme that, as he came once with a sin offering, he should come a second time without a sin offering, that, as he came once to redeem, he should come a second time to claim the inheritance which he has so dearly bought. He came once, that his heel might be bruised; he comes again, to break the serpent's head, and, with a rod of iron, to dash his enemies in pieces, as potters' vessels. He came once, to wear the crown of thorns; he must come again, to wear the diadem of universal dominion. He comes to the marriage supper; he comes to gather his saints together; he comes to glorify them with himself on this same earth where once he and they were despised and rejected of men. Make you sure of this, that the whole drama of redemption cannot be perfected without this last act of the coming of the King. The complete history of paradise regained requires that the New Jerusalem should come down from God out of heaven, prepared as a bride adorned for her husband; and it also requires that the heavenly bridegroom should come riding forth on his white horse, conquering and to conquer, King of kings and Lord of lords, amid the everlasting hallelujahs of saints and angels. It must be so. The man of Nazareth will come again. None shall spit in his face then; but every knee shall bow before him. The crucified shall come again; and though the nail prints will be visible, no nails shall then fasten his dear hands to the tree; but instead thereof, he shall grasp the scepter of universal sovereignty; and he shall reign forever and ever. Hallelujah!

When will he come? Ah, that is the question, the question of questions! He will come in his own time. *He will come in due time.* A brother minister, calling upon me, said, as we sat together, "I should like to ask you a lot of questions about the future." "Oh, well!" I replied, "I cannot answer you, for I daresay I know no more about it than you do." "But," said he, "what about the Lord's second advent? Will there not be the millennium first?" I said, "I cannot tell whether there will be the millennium first; but this I know, the Scripture has left the whole matter, as far as I can see, with an intentional indistinctness, that we may be always expecting Christ to come, and that we may be watching for his coming at any hour and every hour. I think that the millennium will commence after his coming, and not before it. I cannot imagine the kingdom with the King absent. It seems to me to be an essential part of the millennial glory that the King shall then be revealed; at the same time, I am not going to lay down anything definite upon that point. He may not come for a thousand years; he may come tonight. The teaching of Scripture is, first of all, 'In such an hour as ye think not the Son of man cometh.' It is clear that, if it were revealed that a thousand years must elapse before he would come, we might very well go to sleep for that time, for we should have no reason to expect that he would come when Scripture told us he would not."

"Well," answered my friend, "but when Christ comes, that will be the general judgment, will it not?" Then I quoted these texts, "The dead in Christ shall rise first." "But the rest of the dead lived not again until the thousand years were finished. This is the first resurrection." I said, "There is a resurrection from among the dead to which the apostle Paul labored to attain. We shall all rise; but the righteous shall rise a thousand years before the ungodly. There is to be that interval of time between the one and the other; whether that is the millennial glory, or not, this deponent says not, though he thinks it is. But this is the main point, the Lord shall come. We know not when we are to expect his coming; we are not to lay down, as absolutely fixed, any definite prediction or circumstance that would allow us to go to sleep until that prediction was fulfilled, or that circumstance was apparent."

"Will not the Jews be converted to Christ, and restored to their land?" inquired my friend. I replied, "Yes, I think so. Surely they shall look on him whom they have pierced, and they shall mourn for him, as one mourns for his only son; and God shall give them the kingdom and the glory, for they are his people, whom he has not forever cast away. The Jews, who are the natural olive branches, shall yet be grafted into their own olive tree again, and then shall be the fullness of the Gentiles." "Will that be before Christ comes, or after?" asked my friend. I answered, "I think it will be after he comes; but whether or no, I am not going to commit myself to any definite opinion on the subject."

To you, my dear friends, I say, read for yourselves and search for yourselves; for still this stands first and is the only thing that I will insist upon tonight: the Lord will come. He may come now; he may come tomorrow; he may come in the first watch of the night, or the second watch, or he may wait until the morning watch; but the one word that he gives to you all is, "Watch! Watch! Watch!," that whenever he shall come, you may be ready to open to him, and to say, in the language of the hymn we sang just now—

> *Hallelujah!*
> *Welcome, welcome, Judge divine!*

So far I know that we are scriptural, and therefore perfectly safe in our statements about the Lord's second advent.

Brethren, I would be earnest on this point, *for the notion of the delay of Christ's coming is always harmful,* however you arrive at it, whether it be by studying prophecy, or in any other way. If you come to be of the opinion of the servant mentioned in the forty-fifth verse, you are wrong: "If that servant say in his heart, 'My lord delayeth his coming'; and shall begin to beat the menservants and maidens, and to eat and drink, and to be drunken; the lord of that servant will come in a day when he looketh not for him, and at an hour when he is not aware, and will cut him in sunder, and will appoint him his portion with the unbelievers." Do not, therefore, get the idea that the Lord delays his coming, and that he will not or cannot come as yet. Far better would it be for you to stand on the tiptoe of expectation, and to be rather disappointed to think that he does not come. I do not wish you to be shaken in mind so as to act fanatically or foolishly, as certain people did in America, when they went out into the woods with ascension dresses on, so as to go straight up all of a sudden. Fall into none of those absurd ideas that have led people to leave a chair vacant at the table, and to put an empty plate, because the Lord might come and want it; and try to avoid all other superstitious nonsense. To stand stargazing at the prophecies, with your mouth wide open, is just the wrong thing; far better will it be to go on working for your Lord, getting yourself and your service ready for his appearing, and cheering yourself all the while with this thought, "While I am at work, my Master may come. Before I get weary, my Master may return. While others are mocking at me, my Master may appear; and whether they mock or applaud, is nothing to me. I live before the great Taskmaster's eye, and do my service knowing that he sees me, and expecting that, by and by, he will reveal himself to me, and then he will reveal me and my right intention to misrepresenting men." That is the first point, brethren, the Lord will come. Settle that in your minds. He will come in his own time, and we are always to be looking for his appearing.

## 2. Now, second, *the Lord bids us watch for him.*

That is the marrow of the text: "Blessed are those servants, whom the lord when he cometh shall find watching."

Now what is this watching? Not wishing to use my own words, I thought that I would call your attention to the context. The first essential part of this watching is that we are not to be taken up with present things. You remember that the twenty-second verse is about not taking thought what you shall eat, or what you shall drink; you are not to be absorbed in that. You who are Christians are not to live the fleshly, selfish life that asks, "What shall I eat and drink? How can I store up my goods? How can I get food and raiment here?" You are something more than dumb, driven cattle, that must think of hay and water. You have immortal spirits. Rise to the dignity of your immortality. Begin to think of the kingdom, the kingdom so soon to come, the kingdom which your Father has given you, and which, therefore, you must certainly inherit, the kingdom which Christ has prepared for you, and for which he is making you kings and priests unto God, that you may reign with him forever and ever. Oh, be not earthbound! Do not cast your anchor here in these troubled waters. Build not your nest on any of these trees; they are all marked for the ax, and are coming down; and your nest will come down, too, if you build it here. Set your affection on things above, up yonder—

> *Up where eternal ages roll,*
> *Where solid pleasures never die,*
> *And fruits eternal feast the soul;*

there project your thoughts and your anxieties, and have a care about the world to come. Be not anxious about the things that pertain to this life. "Seek ye first the kingdom of God, and his righteousness; and all these things shall be added unto you."

Reading further down, in the thirty-fifth verse, you will notice that watching implies *keeping ourselves in a serviceable condition:* "Let your loins be girded about." You know how the Orientals wear flowing robes, which are always getting in their way. They cannot walk without being tripped up; so that, if a man has a piece of work on hand, he just tucks in his robe under his girdle, ties his girdle up tightly, and gets ready for his task; as we should say in English, turning the Oriental into the western figure, rolling up your shirtsleeves, and preparing for work. That is the way to wait for the Lord, ready for service, that, when he comes, he may never find you idle. I called to see a sister one morning; and when I called, she was cleaning the front steps with some whitening, and she said, "Oh, my dear pastor, I am sorry that you should call upon me just now! I would not have had you see me like this on any account." I answered, "That is how I like to see you, busy at your work. I should not have liked to have come in, and caught you talking to your neighbor over the back palings. That would not have pleased me at all. May your Lord, when he comes, find you just so, doing your duty!" You see exactly what is meant; you are to be doing your duty; you are to be engaged about those vocations to which God has called you. You are to be doing it all out of love to Christ, and as service for him. Oh, that we might watch in that style, with our loins girded about! Work and wait and watch! Can you put those three things together? Work and wait and watch! This is what your Master asks of you.

And next, he would have us wait with our lights burning. If the Master comes home late, let us sit up late for him. It is not for us to go to bed till he comes home. Have the lights all trimmed; have his chamber well lit up; have the entrance hall ready for his approach. When the King comes, have your torches flaming, that you may go out to meet the royal bridegroom, and escort him to his home. If we are to watch for the Lord, as we ought, it must be with lamps burning. Are you making your light to shine among men? Do you think that your conduct and character are an example that will do your neighbors good, and are you trying to teach others the way of salvation? Some professors are like dark lanterns, or candles under a bushel. May we never be such! May we stand with our lamps trimmed, and our lights burning, and we ourselves like unto men that wait for their Lord; not walking in darkness, nor concealing our light, but letting it shine brightly! That is the way to watch for Christ, with your girdle tight about you because you are ready for work, and your lamp flaming out with brightness because you are anxious to illuminate the dark world in which you live.

To put it very plainly, I think that watching for the coming of the Lord means acting just as you would wish to be acting if he were to come. I saw, in the orphanage schoolroom, that little motto, "What would Jesus do?" That is a very splendid motto for our whole life. "What would Jesus do in such a case and in such a case?" Do just that. Another good motto is, "What would Jesus think of me if he were to come?" There are some places into which a Christian could not go, for he would not like his Master to find him there. There are some kinds of amusements into which a believer would never enter, for he would be ashamed for his Master to come and find him there. There are some conditions of angry temper, of pride, petulance, or spiritual sloth, in which you would not like to be if you felt that the Master was coming. Suppose an angel's wing should brush your cheek just as you have spoken some unkind word, and a voice should say, "Your Master is coming," you would tremble, I am sure, to meet him in such a condition. O beloved, let us try every morning to get up as if that were the morning in which Christ would come; and when we go up to bed at night, may we lie down with this thought, "Perhaps I shall be awakened by the ringing out of the silver trumpets heralding his coming. Before the sun arises, I may be startled from my dreams by the greatest of all cries, 'The Lord is come! The Lord is come!'" What a check, what an incentive, what a bridle, what a spur, such thoughts as these would be to us! Take this for the guide of your whole life. Act as if Jesus would come during the act in which you are engaged; and if you would not wish to be caught in that act by the coming of the Lord, let it not be your act.

The second verse of our text speaks about the Master coming in the second watch, or in the third watch. *We are to act as those who keep the watches of the age for Christ.* Among the Romans, it was as it is on board ship; there were certain watches. A Roman soldier, perhaps, stood on guard for three hours, and when he had been on the watch for three hours, there came another sentry who took his place, and the first man retired, and went back to the barracks, and the fresh sentinel stood in his place during his allotted time. Brethren, we have succeeded a long line of watchmen. Since the days of our Lord, when he sent out the chosen twelve to stand upon the citadel, and tell how the night waxed or waned, how have the watchers come and gone! Our God has changed the watchers, but he has kept the watch. He still sets watchmen on the walls of Zion, who cannot hold their peace day or night, but must watch for the coming of their master, watch against evil times, watch against error, and watch for the souls of men. At this time, some of us are called to be specially on the watch, and dare we sleep? After such a line of lynx-eyed watchmen, who counted not their lives dear unto them that they might hold their post, and watch against the foe, shall we be cravens, and be afraid; or shall we be sluggards, and go to our beds? By him that lives and was dead and is alive forevermore, we pray that we may never be guilty of treason to his sacred name and truth; but may we watch on to the last moment when there shall ring out the clarion cry, "Behold, the bridegroom cometh; go ye out to meet him." People of the tabernacle, you are set to watch tonight just as they did in the brave days of old! Whitefield and Wesley's men were watchers; and those before them, in the days of Luther and of Calvin, and backward even to the days of our Lord. They kept the watches of the night, and you must do the same, until—

> *Upstarting at the midnight cry,*
> *"Behold your heavenly bridegroom nigh,"*

you go forth to welcome your returning Lord.

We are to wait with one object in view, namely, *to open the door to him, and to welcome him*: "that when he cometh and knocketh, they may open unto him immediately." Perhaps you know what it is to go home to a loving, tender wife and children who are watching for you. You have been on a journey; you have been absent for some little time; you have written them letters which they have greatly valued; you have heard from them; but all that is nothing like your personal presence. They are looking out for you; and if, perchance, the boat should fail you, or the train be late, if you arrived at eleven or twelve o'clock at night, you would not expect to find the house all shut up, and nobody watching for you. No, you had told them that you would come, and you were quite sure that they would watch for you. I feel rebuked myself, sometimes, for not watching for my Master, when I know that, at this very time, my dogs are sitting against the door, waiting for me; and long before I reach home, there they will be, and at the first sound of the carriage wheels, they will lift up their voices with delight because their master is coming home. Oh, if we loved our Lord as dogs love their masters, how we should catch the first sound of his coming, and be waiting, always waiting, and never happy until at last we should see him! Pardon me for using a dog as a picture of what you ought to be; but when you have attained to a state above that, I will find another illustration to explain my meaning.

### 3. Now, lastly, *there is a reward for watchers.*

Their reward is this, "Blessed are those servants, whom the lord when he cometh shall find watching."

*They have a present blessedness.* It is a very blessed thing to be on the watch for Christ, it is a blessing to us now. How it detaches you from the world! You can be poor without murmuring; you can be rich without worldliness; you can be sick without sorrowing; you can be healthy without presumption. If you are always waiting for Christ's coming, untold blessings are wrapped up in that glorious hope. "Every man that hath this hope in him purifieth himself even as he is pure." Blessednesses are heaped up one upon another in that state of heart in which a man is always looking for his Lord.

But what will be the blessedness when Jesus does come? Well, a part of that blessedness will be *in future service.* You must not think that, when you have done working here, you Sunday school teachers, and those of us who preach and teach, that the Master will say, "I have discharged you from my service. Go and sit on a heavenly mount, and sing yourselves away forever and ever." Not a bit of it. I am but learning how to preach now; I shall be able to preach by and by. You are only learning to teach now; you will be able to teach by and by. Yes, to angels and principalities and powers, you shall make known the manifold wisdom of God. I sometimes aspire to the thought of a congregation of angels and archangels, who shall sit and wonder, as I tell what God has done for me; and I shall be to them an everlasting monument of the grace of God to an unworthy wretch, upon whom he looked with infinite compassion and saved with a wonderful salvation. All those stars, those worlds of light, who knows how many of them are inhabited? I believe there are regions beyond our imagination to which every child of God shall become an everlasting illumination, a living example of the love of God in Christ Jesus. The people in those far distant lands could not see Calvary as this world has seen it; but they shall hear of it from the redeemed. Remember how the Lord will say, "Well done, thou good and faithful servant: thou hast been faithful over a few things, I will make thee ruler over many things." He is to keep on doing something, you see. Instead of having some little bit of a village to govern, he is to be made ruler over some great province. So it is in this passage. Read the forty-fourth verse: "Of a truth I say unto you, that he will make him ruler over all that he hath." That is, the man who has been a faithful and wise steward of

God here will be called of God to more eminent service hereafter. If he serves his Master well, when his Master comes, he will promote him to still higher service. Do you not know how it used to be in the Spartan army? Here is a man who has fought well, and been a splendid soldier. He is covered with wounds on his breast. The next time that there is a war, they say, "Poor fellow, we will reward him! He shall lead the way in the first battle. He fought so well before, when he met one hundred with a little troop behind him; now he shall meet ten thousand with a larger troop." "Oh!" say you, "that is giving him more work." That is God's way of rewarding his people, and a blessed thing it is for the industrious servant. His rest is in serving God with all his might. This shall be our heaven, not to go there to roost, but to be always on the wing; forever flying, and forever resting at the same time. "They do his commandments, hearkening unto the voice of his word." "His servants shall serve him: and they shall see his face." These two things blended together make a noble ambition for every Christian.

May the Lord keep you waiting, working, watching, that when he comes, you may have the blessedness of entering upon some larger, higher, nobler service than you could accomplish now, for which you are preparing by the lowlier and more arduous service of this world! God bless you, beloved, and if any of you do not know my Lord, and therefore do not look for his appearing, remember that he will come whether you look for him or not; and when he comes, you will have to stand at his bar. One of the events that will follow his coming will be your being summoned before his judgment seat, and how will you answer him then? How will you answer him if you have refused his love and turned a deaf ear to the invitations of his mercy? If you have delayed and delayed and delayed and delayed, how will you answer him? How will you answer him in that day? If you stand speechless, your silence will condemn you, and the King will say, "Bind him hand and foot, and take him away." God grant that we may believe in the Lord Jesus unto life eternal, and then wait for his appearing from heaven, for his love's sake! Amen.

# Index to Key Scriptures

| | | |
|---|---|---|
| Matthew 16:28 | *An Awful Premonition* | 1 |
| Matthew 25:31–36 | *The Reward of the Righteous* | 15 |
| Luke 12:37–38 | *Watching for Christ's Coming* | 154 |
| Acts 1:10–11 | *The Ascension and the Advent Practically Considered* | 70 |
| Romans 2:16 | *Coming Judgment of the Secrets of Men* | 84 |
| 2 Corinthians 5:10 | *The Great Assize* | 43 |
| Philippians 3:20–4:1 | *The Watchword for Today: "Stand Fast"* | 112 |
| 2 Thessalonians 1:10 | *Jesus Admired in Them That Believe* | 55 |
| Titus 2:11–14 | *The Two Appearings and the Discipline of Grace* | 98 |
| 1 John 2:28 | *Preparation for the Coming of the Lord* | 140 |
| Revelation 1:7 | *"He Cometh with Clouds"* | 126 |
| Revelation 20:11 | *The Great White Throne* | 29 |

# Timeless wisdom for your spiritual journey.
## Collect all sixteen.

### • Sermons On •

- The Lord's Supper
- Men of the New Testament
- Women of the New Testament
- Men of the Old Testament
- Women of the Old Testament
- Heaven and Hell
- Great Prayers of the Bible
- Prayer
- The Second Coming of Christ
- The Prayers of Christ
- Christmas
- The Love of Christ
- The Holy Spirit
- Cries from the Cross
- The Passion of Christ
- The Resurrection

**HENDRICKSON PUBLISHERS**